WILD WEATHER

Sandy Creek

Copyright © QEB Publishing 2008

This 2009 edition published by Sandy Creek by arrangement with QEB Publishing, Inc.

Library of Congress Cataloging-in-Publication Data

Vaughan, Jenny
  Blizzards / Jenny Vaughan.
    p. cm. -- (Wild weather)
  Includes index.
  Summary: "Discusses blizzards, heat waves, floods, hurricanes , and tornadoes where they are common, how they affect us, and how people cope with them"--Provided by publisher.
  ISBN 978-1-59566-586-7
 1. Blizzards--Juvenile literature. I. Title.
 QC926.37.R69 2009
 551.55'5--dc22

                                        2008012591

Vaughan, Jenny.
  Heat waves / Jenny Vaughan
 1. Heat waves (Meteorology)--Juvenile literature. I. Title.
 QC981.8.A5R69 2009
 551.5'253--dc22

                                        2008012596

Royston, Angela.
  Hurricanes and tornadoes / Angela Royston.
 1. Hurricanes--Juvenile literature. 2. Tornadoes--Juvenile literature. I. Title.
 QC944.R69 2009
 551.55'2--dc22

                                        2008012598

Royston, Angela.
  Floods / Angela Royston.
    p. cm. -- (Wild weather)
 1. Floods--Juvenile literature. I. Title.
 GB1399.R68 2009
 551.48'9--dc22

                                        2008012594

Authors Angela Royston and Jenny Vaughan
Consultant Terry Jennings
Editor Amanda Askew
Designer Mo Choy
Picture Researcher Claudia Tate
Illustrator Julian Baker

Publisher Steve Evans
Creative Director Zeta Davies
Managing Editor Amanda Askew

Sandy Creek
122 Fifth Avenue
New York, NY 10011

ISBN: 978 1 4351 2034 1

Printed and bound in China

10 9 8 7 6 5 4 3 2 1

Words in **bold** can be found in the glossary on pages 32, 60, 88, and 116.

Contents

Floods

Hurricanes and Tornadoes

HEAT WAVE

What is a heat wave?

A heat wave is a long period of unusually hot weather. Like other forms of extreme weather, it can affect the environment and human health.

WEATHER AND CLIMATE

WEATHER is...

wind—movement of the air

visibility—how far we can see in the air

precipitation—rain, snow, or hail

temperature—how hot or cold the air is (measured in degrees Celsius, °C, or degrees Fahrenheit, °F)

CLIMATE is the average weather a place gets over a long period of time.

RISING TEMPERATURES

A heat wave happens when a mass of unusually warm air stays still over the same place for days or even weeks, with no cooler weather. In parts of the world where the weather is frequently very warm, hot weather is not considered to be a heat wave. Elsewhere, the same temperatures, or even lower ones, are a heat wave, just because they are not normal.

▼ In Brazil, temperatures are about 86°F (30°C) on average in summer. Although this is very warm, it is normal for this area and people have adapted to the climate.

◄ Hot weather and low rainfall have led to low water levels in the San Gabriel Reservoir, California.

THE HEAT INDEX

High temperatures combined with high **humidity** make hot weather seem even hotter. The U.S. government uses its **Heat Index** to calculate how air temperature will feel. Air temperature and humidity are measured, and then whether the measurement is in or out of direct sunlight is taken into consideration. The U.S. government warns the public when it expects the Heat Index to reach 105.8°F (41°C) or more for at least two days in a row.

◄ Qingdao, China, during a spell of hot weather in 2006. When the weather is hot, people often crowd onto beaches to enjoy the warmth and sunshine.

Where is hot weather most common?

Places along the **Equator** have the warmest climates. These areas are called the **tropics** and they have tropical climates. Daytime temperatures can reach around 95°F (35°C) throughout the year. However, these temperatures are normal, so they are not a heat wave.

RECORD HEATWAVE

In the summer of 1923 to 1924, the temperature in Marble Bar, Australia, reached more than 100 °F (38°C) for 160 days in a row. Marble Bar often gets high temperatures, but this was a world record.

▼ The different climates of the world. The warmest areas are those nearest the Equator.

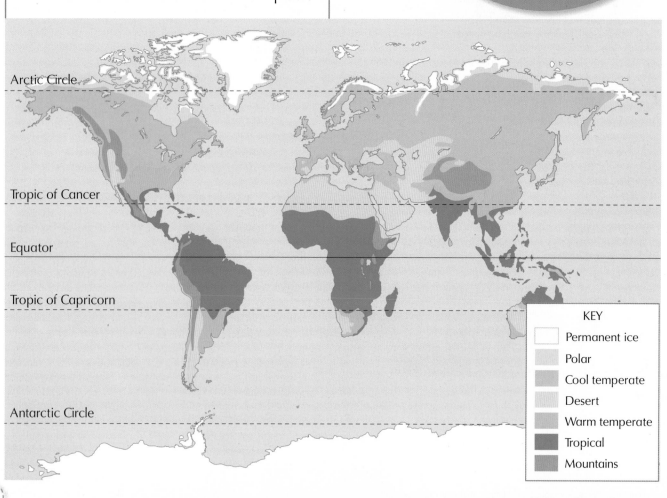

Arctic Circle

Tropic of Cancer

Equator

Tropic of Capricorn

Antarctic Circle

KEY
- Permanent ice
- Polar
- Cool temperate
- Desert
- Warm temperate
- Tropical
- Mountains

TROPICAL CLIMATES

Some tropical climates are the most humid climates in the world. They have heavy rainfall, especially at certain times of the year, and they feel sticky and uncomfortable most of the time. Even at night, temperatures may never drop much below 71°F (22°C) because thick clouds hold the heat from the Sun close to the Earth's surface. This happens in the great tropical rain forests, such as those around the Amazon River in Brazil, the Congo River in West Africa, and in Indonesia. Other tropical climates are drier, at least for part of the year. In these areas, there are often vast areas of grassland, such as in the African savanna.

▲ In a tropical rainforest, the warm temperatures and heavy rainfall provide perfect conditions for thick vegetation to grow.

▼ Few plants or animals can survive in the hot, dry environment of Death Valley, California.

HOT DESERTS

A **desert** is where the climate is very dry, so little can grow. Deserts close to the Equator, such as the Sahara Desert in Africa, can have some of the highest daytime temperatures in the world— more than 122°F (50°C). The highest recorded temperature was 136°F (50°C) in El Azizia, Libya, on September 13, 1922. Desert temperatures may drop sharply at night because there are few clouds to trap the warm air near the Earth's surface.

Why do some places get warm weather?

The main factors that affect how warm a place normally gets are the **latitude**, the **altitude**, how far from the ocean it is, and the time of year.

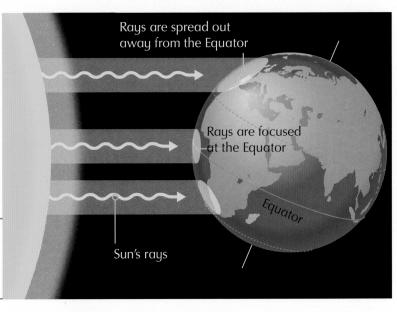

Rays are spread out away from the Equator

Rays are focused at the Equator

Equator

Sun's rays

▶ Close to the Equator, the Sun is very strong, which makes the weather warmer.

▼ Although Mount Kilimanjaro, Tanzania, lies close to the Equator, its summit, or top, is covered in snow.

LATITUDE

Latitude is how far north or south of the Equator a place is. Near the Equator, it is hotter because the Sun's rays reach the Earth most directly there. Further from the Equator, the rays strike the Earth at an angle, so they are more spread out and not as strong.

ALTITUDE

Altitude measures how high above sea level the land is. At high altitudes, the air is cooler than lower down. The temperature at the foot of a mountain can be very warm, but it may never be warm at the top.

WIND AND WATER

Land warms up faster than water. The warm air above the land rises. Near the coast, cooler air from the sea moves in to take its place, keeping coastal areas cool. Inland, away from the cool sea winds, air temperatures tend to be higher.

SEASONS

The **seasons** winter and summer occur because the Earth is tilted slightly on its **axis** as it travels on its yearly journey around the Sun. For part of the year, the northern half is closer to the Sun, and it is summer there. As the Earth continues on its journey, the southern half tilts toward the Sun, so it is summer in the south and winter in the north.

▼ Wind occurs when warm air rises and cooler air moves across the Earth's surface to take its place.

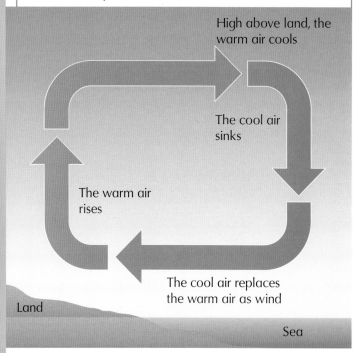

High above land, the warm air cools

The cool air sinks

The warm air rises

The cool air replaces the warm air as wind

Land

Sea

▼ The Earth is tilted on its axis. Temperatures are warmer when the Earth tilts toward the Sun. At this time, it is summer.

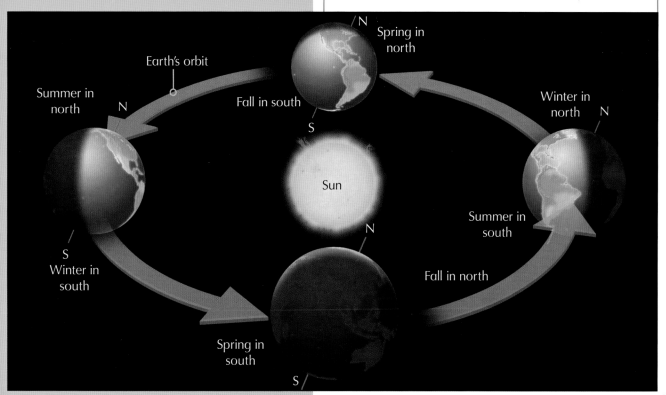

Earth's orbit

Summer in north

Spring in north

Fall in south

Winter in north

Winter in south

Summer in south

Spring in south

Fall in north

Sun

What causes a heat wave?

The Earth is surrounded by a blanket of air called the **atmosphere**. The atmosphere is in layers, and the weather happens in the bottom layer. During a heat wave, warm air becomes "stuck" over a region of the Earth's surface, leading to long periods with high temperatures.

◄ The Earth is surrounded by a blanket of air called the atmosphere. This is where weather takes place.

STATIONARY AIR

Normally, as the Sun warms the Earth, the air above it warms and rises. Cooler winds rush in, bringing rain, which helps to cool the Earth's surface and the air above it. If the warm air remains stationary, it blocks cool air and rain—and a heat wave occurs.

► During a heat wave, warm air remains over a region for days on end, with no cooler air, clouds, or rain to bring the temperature down.

▼ The long period of hot, dry weather that results in a heatwave also means that river levels will drop. Nuclear **power stations** that use river water to cool their reactors cannot work fully when this happens.

HEATWAVE IN FRANCE

In July and August 2003, a heat wave struck Europe, with temperatures reaching up to 104°F (40°C) for more than 20 days. In France, many nuclear power stations had to close. The river water that was needed to cool the reactors became too warm and too low.

▼ It is essential to drink lots of fresh water during a heat wave to keep the body hydrated.

HOW DOES HUMIDITY AFFECT US IN A HEAT WAVE?

When humans **sweat**, water in the body passes out through the skin and **evaporates** to cool the body down. However, when it is humid, there is already a lot of moisture in the air, so the air cannot absorb much more. Therefore, when humans sweat, it remains on the skin, making us feel sticky and uncomfortable. Our skin cannot cool down, so we feel much hotter.

Modern life

Many ways have been found to cope with the problems that unusual weather can bring, but very hot weather can still make modern life difficult.

▼ **Photochemical smog** hovers over El Paso, Texas. This white mist is caused by sunlight reacting with car exhaust fumes.

SMOG

When warm air is trapped over a city, strong sunlight reacts with gases from car exhausts and forms a thick, white mist called photochemical smog. This can hurt people's eyes and cause breathing problems. Today, new cars are usually made so that their exhausts give off fewer harmful gases.

▲ Sticky, melted tarmac from roads and sidewalks is impossible to remove from anything it clings to.

URBAN HEAT ISLANDS

Cities tend to be much hotter than the countryside around them. These are called "urban **heat islands**." They form because the bricks and concrete of a city absorb heat from the Sun during the day, and then release it at night. This keeps temperatures high and allows a steady build-up of heat. Lack of wind and the heat given out by air conditioning systems and other machinery add to this effect. In Chicago in July 1995, temperatures reached 105°F (41°C) by day and only dropped to 84°F (29°C) at night. This led to more than 500 deaths in five days.

RAIL AND ROAD

Driving in hot weather can be dangerous because roads can become damaged. **Tarmac** melts and car tires can burst on extremely hot surfaces. Metal expands when it is hot, which causes great problems on the railroads. In the past, rails were short, with small spaces between them, so that they could expand safely. Today, they are longer, without the spaces. The metal is treated and laid in ways that help to stop the rails expanding too much. However, if the metal does expand, it has no space to move into, and may be forced out of shape. If this happens, trains cannot use the rails, as there is a risk of accidents.

▼ This aerial picture shows the heat given off by buildings in an urban area in red. The cooler vegetation areas are shown in green.

Wildfires

In hot, dry weather, trees and grasslands become very dry. Wildfires, or forest fires, can easily start and spread very quickly.

▼ A wildfire threatens beachside homes in Malibu, California, in 1993.

HOW A WILDFIRE SPREADS

Wildfires are sometimes started on purpose, but they are mainly the result of mistakes—for example when someone drops a cigarette. If grass, or the sticks and leaves on the forest floor, are dry, they can soon catch fire. In hot weather, such fires will burn even more easily. Once it has started, a wildfire spreads rapidly as embers and sparks are carried on the wind. It can be extremely difficult for firefighters to stop the flames spreading. Nearby trees and grass soon catch fire so, as soon as one fire is under control, another may break out close by.

▶ A firebreak in New Zealand has been made by cutting down a strip of trees in the middle of the forest.

PREVENTING FIRES

In some countries, when the weather is hot and dry, special warnings remind people not to take risks. Camp fires, barbecues, and smoking in the countryside may be forbidden. Sometimes, strips of forest are cut down to make spaces that the fires cannot cross. These are called **firebreaks**.

HELP AT HAND

Fighting wildfires can be too much for local emergency services. They often need help from other parts of their country—or even from abroad. In 2007, the Greek fire services were helped by Russian "water-bomber" aircraft. Each plane can release 42 tons of water over a fire—as much as 525 bathtubs!

GREEK TRAGEDY

In the summer of 2007, temperatures in southern Europe reached more than 104 degrees Fahrenheit for many days, with little rain. In southern Greece, there were nearly 200 forest fires on the dry hillsides. More than 60 people died and firefighters came from across Europe to help put out the flames.

▼ A low-flying aircraft drops fire retardant onto the wildfire to try to put out and control the flames.

Human health

Heat waves are one of the most dangerous kinds of extreme weather. U.S. government figures show that more people die from the effects of heat than from any other natural disaster.

HEAT STRESS

In hot weather, it important to keep cool by staying in the shade, wearing light-colored clothes, and drinking plenty of clean water. This helps to avoid health problems called **heat stress**. This can include cramps, **heat exhaustion** and, most seriously, **heat stroke**.

HEAT STROKE

Heat stroke occurs when the body's temperature rises dangerously. If body temperature rises above 104°F (40°C) and it cannot be cooled, a person may go into a coma and die. Also, high temperatures and not being able to sleep during hot nights can put a strain on the heart.

◀ For older people with weak hearts and poor blood circulation, high temperatures bring an increased risk of heat stroke.

OTHER HEALTH PROBLEMS

People who sunbathe may burn their skin if they do not use **sunscreen**. In the long term, this can result in skin cancer. Diseases, such as **malaria**, are also spread by insects that breed in hot climates. Stomach problems can also be caused by hot weather because germs breed in food that is going bad. In poor countries, a heat wave results in a shortage of clean drinking water. People may be forced to drink water full of germs that cause killer diseases, such as **cholera**.

▲ Sunscreen filters out the harmful rays from the Sun, and helps to prevent sunburn and long-term damage to the skin.

SAFETY IN HOT WEATHER

Drink plenty of fluids to make up for the moisture your body loses as you sweat. Close blinds and curtains to shade rooms, and open windows to let fresh air in.

▲ Certain kinds of mosquito that live in hot climates can carry malaria. This is a dangerous disease that kills up to two million people a year.

Food and farming

Animals and plants also suffer during a heat wave. Often they cannot find water or food, and without shade, there is no escape from the heat.

▲ Animals in zoos are often given their food in blocks of ice. This helps them to stay cool.

KEEPING ANIMALS COOL

Animals can die from heat stroke, too. During a heat wave in California in 2006, temperatures rose to more than 114°F (46°C). Farmers had to find ways of keeping their animals cool, including giving them showers. However, more than 25,000 cattle and 700,000 chickens died. In the end, the estimated cost of the heat wave to farmers was more than one billion dollars.

SUNSCREEN FOR SHEEP

Sheep can also suffer in hot weather, especially just after they have been sheared because they have no wool. In Australia, sunscreen has been invented to protect their skin until a new coat grows.

A farmer in South Carolina examines his **crops**, which have been killed by a period of very hot, dry weather.

WILTING PLANTS

Plants can be affected in hot weather. Lettuce leaves may burn, or the whole plant may "bolt" —the stems grow long and the lettuce leaves turn bitter, so they cannot be eaten. Tomatoes and other fruits and vegetables may be scorched. If temperatures are very high, some fruits, such as plums, stop growing, and so the crop is small.

ALGAE

Some living things do very well in hot weather, and this may also be harmful. For example, huge quantities of tiny plants called algae may form in stagnant water. They produce a thick, green scum on the surface. Some kinds of algae are poisonous.

◄ In hot weather, the amount of **duckweed**, a small plant, can double in size daily. In 2006, it covered more than 5 miles of a canal in London, England.

Drought

A **drought** is a long period of time without rain. The ground becomes dry and crops, animals, and people can die from lack of water.

WATER SHORTAGE

During a drought, more water is used, especially when temperatures are high. Crops and plants are in danger of dying unless they are watered. Governments advise people to save water in case shortages occur. For example, people are sometimes forbidden from using hosepipes because they waste water quickly. Every drop of water is needed for washing and drinking and to keep farm animals and crops alive.

▲ In dry parts of the world, wind-driven pumps bring water up from underground **boreholes**.

◄ In parts of Africa, a drought can mean that everyone must help to bring water from distant streams and wells.

During a drought, rivers may appear to dry out completely. However, it may be possible to find water under the surface of the **riverbed**.

YEARS OF DROUGHT

In countries where droughts are common, people may harvest, or save, water during the rainy times. In one region in Zimbabwe, Africa, villagers have cut underground tanks out of the rocks to store rainwater. However, when a drought goes on for a long time, there is a limit to what people can do to overcome the problems. By April 2007, after several very dry years, Australia began to suffer greatly. Farmers needed help from the government to keep their farms going. Water in one of the country's main rivers, the Murray-Darling, was too low to flow out to sea properly. In some places, kangaroos came into people's gardens to look for food and water.

Heat and wildlife

Some plants and animals are adapted to live in hot, dry climates. They have developed ways to survive when other living things would find the conditions very difficult.

▼ The fennec fox uses its huge ears to keep cool. Blood flows through vessels in the ears and is cooled down by the air, keeping the fox's body temperature down.

ANIMALS

Many desert animals are nocturnal, remaining hidden underground during the heat of the day. In the summer, some animals lose part of their coat—this is called molting. Some frogs and turtles **aestivate**, or sleep. They wake up when cooler, wetter weather arrives.

▼ Fish crowd into the shallows in a **reservoir** near Los Angeles. High temperatures can lead to a loss of **oxygen** from water. Fish become distressed and may die in large numbers.

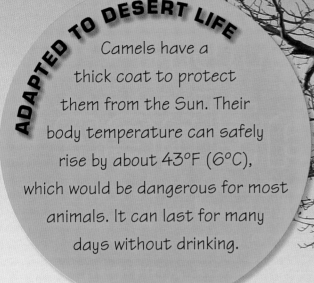

PLANTS

Many tropical plants have thick, waxy leaves so that they do not lose much moisture through evaporation. Others, such as **cacti**, store water in their swollen stems. The baobab tree grows in Africa and other hot, dry parts of the world. A mature baobab can store more than 31,700 gallons (120,00 liters) of water in its trunk—that is 700 bathtubs of water! The tree saves water by losing its leaves during the dry part of the year, so that it looks almost dead. When the rains come, it grows leaves, flowers, and then fruit.

▲ Baobab trees in Africa store water in their thick trunks all through the driest part of the year.

Living with hot weather

People who live in hot countries have found ways to protect themselves from high temperatures by adapting their clothing and homes.

CLOTHING

In warm parts of the world, people wear garments that allow air to move around the body. It is best if these are made of absorbent material, such as cotton, which soaks up sweat. Light colors also **reflect** the Sun's rays, whereas dark colors absorb the heat. Where the Sun's rays are very strong, many people keep their skin covered, so that it does not burn.

▼ People who live in the desert protect themselves from the strong rays of the Sun by wearing loose, light-colored clothing.

AIR CONDITIONING

Many modern homes use air conditioning. This is a way of artificially cooling the air before it reaches the inside of a house, in a similar way to a refrigerator. Air conditioning uses a lot of electricity, so in a heat wave, power cuts may occur.

HOMES

Traditional homes are often designed to keep people comfortable. Thick mud or stone walls prevent heat from the outside world entering the home. Small windows on both sides of a building keep out as much sunshine as possible, while allowing air to flow through the building.

▼ In Coober Pedy, Australia, many homes are built underground. They remain cool during summer, when average temperatures are above 86°F (30°C).

▼ The white walls of homes in countries such as Greece reflect the heat, keeping the houses cool inside. **Shutters** on the windows provide shade and allow air to pass through them.

Knock-on effects

Periods of unusually warm weather can cause long-term damage to the way plants and animals live together and depend on each other. When this happens, the **ecosystem** in which the animal or plant lives is harmed.

CORAL REEFS

Colorful coral reefs are home to large numbers of fish and other wildlife. People depend on this wildlife for food, and also for the money they get from tourists who visit the reefs.

▼ Coral is normally covered with colorful algae. However, when the seawater around it becomes too warm, the algae die, leaving the coral white in color.

COMPLICATED ECOSYSTEMS

Coral reefs are made up tiny living things, covered by colorful algae. The algae are also living creatures and they provide food for the coral. If the water is too warm, the algae leave and the coral turns white. When the water cools, the algae may return. However, if the temperature remains just two degrees Fahrenheit above normal for more than a couple of months, the coral starts to die and the damage is permanent.

▼ If birds nest too early in the year due to warmer weather, the young birds will suffer if temperatures return to normal.

SEASONS OUT OF CONTROL

In cooler parts of the world, warmer weather in winter can damage ecosystems. Warm weather may encourage birds to nest and rear young early, before there are enough insects to feed on. If the weather turns cold again, the young may die.

▼ A spring heat wave can bring early blossom, which can be damaged if cold temperatures return.

FRUIT FARMS

Warm winter weather can create all sorts of problems for fruit farmers. If temperatures are high, some trees may come into bloom early. Then cold temperatures may suddenly return. Blossom may die, without ever being able to form fruit later in the year.

Are heat waves getting worse?

The Earth's climate is getting warmer. This is called **global warming**. It has been happening at a greater speed in recent years. Scientists believe that the rising amount of **greenhouses gases** is the cause.

Sun's rays are reflected

Heat escapes

Sun's rays

Sun's rays are trapped, which warms the atmosphere

▲ The Sun warms the Earth and certain gases, such as carbon dioxide, trap some of the heat in the atmosphere. They act like the glass in a greenhouse.

GREENHOUSE GASES

The Sun heats the Earth's surface, which then warms the air above it. Greenhouse gases in the air trap this heat—similar to the way a greenhouse traps heat. Humans are burning large amounts of **fossil fuels**—coal, gas, and oil. This produces **carbon dioxide**, one of the main greenhouse gases. At the same time, many trees, which absorb carbon dioxide, are being destroyed. Some scientists think that temperatures could rise as much as 44 degrees Fahrenheit in the next 100 years because we are burning too much fuel.

THE FUTURE

Rising temperatures may make weather very unpredictable, with more storms, flooding, and heat waves. Warmer temperatures in the **Arctic** and **Antarctic** have already resulted in much of the ice there melting. This could make sea levels rise, flooding low-lying countries. With higher temperatures, there could be more disease, and it may be harder to grow enough food. Global warming is already happening, but we must try to stop it getting worse.

▼ Global warming could mean that **locusts**, which devastate crops in the tropics, could spread further afield.

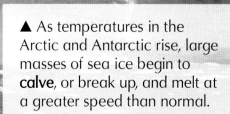

▲ As temperatures in the Arctic and Antarctic rise, large masses of sea ice begin to **calve**, or break up, and melt at a greater speed than normal.

Glossary

AESTIVATE To fall into a kind of deep sleep during hot, dry weather.

ALTITUDE The height above sea level.

ANTARCTIC The region around the South Pole.

ARCTIC The region around the North Pole.

ATMOSPHERE The blanket of air around the Earth.

AXIS An imaginary line through the middle of the Earth from the North Pole to the South Pole.

BOREHOLE A hole drilled deep into the ground to find water or minerals.

CACTUS A desert plant with a thick, fleshy stem.

CALVE When a glacier or sheet of sea ice breaks up, it is calving.

CARBON DIOXIDE One of the gases in the air. Carbon dioxide is produced when fuel is burned.

CHOLERA A disease of the stomach and intestines, with severe diarrhea. Untreated, it can kill very quickly.

CROP Plants grown by farmers to be used in some way, for example, as food.

DESERT A region with little rain and few plants.

DROUGHT A long period without rain, or with very little rain.

DUCKWEED A kind of small plant that grows in still, fresh water.

ECOSYSTEM The way in which animals and plants in a particular area are related to each other and to their environment.

EQUATOR An imaginary line around the middle of the Earth, halfway between the North Pole and the South Pole.

EVAPORATE To change from a liquid into a gas.

FIREBREAK An area of cleared land created to prevent fire from spreading, for example through a forest.

FOSSIL FUELS Coal, oil, and natural gas. These fuels were formed millions of years ago from the remains of plants and marine animals.

GLOBAL WARMING Increase in the average temperature of the air around the Earth. Global warming is caused by an increase in greenhouse gases, such as carbon dioxide, in the air.

GREENHOUSE GAS Gas in the air that traps the Sun's heat. Greenhouse gases include water vapor, carbon dioxide, and methane.

HEAT EXHAUSTION Dizziness, weakness, and other mild health problems that happen when the body is too hot.

HEAT INDEX A way of measuring how hot the air actually feels.

HEAT ISLAND A place where temperatures are higher than in surrounding areas.

HEAT STRESS A range of problems caused by the body becoming too hot. It includes heat exhaustion and heat stroke.

HEAT STROKE Collapse caused by too much heat—the most dangerous form of heat stress.

HUMIDITY The moisture in the air.

LATITUDE The distance a place is north or south of the Equator. It is measured in degrees.

LOCUST A kind of grasshopper. Locusts sometimes gather in huge swarms and destroy crops.

MALARIA A disease caused by parasites that is spread by a type of mosquito. It causes high fever, and can kill.

OXYGEN A gas in the air that living things need in order to survive.

PHOTOCHEMICAL SMOG A mist caused by the action of sunshine on chemicals from car exhausts.

POWER STATION A building in which electricity is generated.

REFLECT To cast back light.

RESERVOIR An artificial lake used for storing water.

RIVERBED A channel in the ground through which a river flows.

SEASON A period of the year, such as spring, summer, fall, and winter. In some parts of the world, there are also wet and dry seasons.

SHUTTERS Movable covers for windows.

SUNSCREEN A skin lotion containing chemicals that can block the harmful rays from the Sun.

SWEAT Moisture that passes out through the skin when we are warm.

TARMAC A road surface made with tar.

TROPICS Part of the world on each side of the Equator between the Tropic of Cancer and the Tropic of Capricorn.

BLIZZARDS

What is a blizzard?

A blizzard is a form of extreme weather, with high winds and heavy snow. Normal life may grind to a halt. Traveling may become impossible, and temperatures can be dangerously low. Even after it is over, a blizzard leaves behind large amounts of snow, often driven by the wind into heaps, called **drifts**.

WIND AND SNOW

A blizzard is more than just heavy snowfall—it is an especially violent snowstorm. The definition of a blizzard used in the United States is a wind of more than 34 miles (56 km) an hour, with enough snow in the air to make it impossible to see for more than 490 ft (150 m). A severe blizzard has winds of more than 44 miles (72 km) an hour with temperatures below 10°F (-12°C). There must also be so much snow in the air that it is impossible to see anything at all.

◄ When heavy snow falls, roads become icy and may even be blocked completely—causing long traffic jams.

▲ Quebec, Canada, lies under a blanket of snow. Although it looks beautiful, cold temperatures and heavy snow bring problems.

WHERE DOES THE WORD "BLIZZARD" COME FROM?

Blizzards have happened for centuries, but the word "blizzard" as a term for a violent snowstorm is quite new. Until the end of the 19th century, it was used to mean cannon shot or musket fire. Then, in the 1870s, a newspaper in Iowa first used it to describe a heavy snowstorm with violent wind. The snow does not actually have to be falling in a blizzard—it may have been lying on the ground, whipped up by the wind.

WEATHER AND CLIMATE

WEATHER is...
wind—movement of the air
visibility—how far we can see in the air
precipitation—rain, snow, or hail
temperature—how hot or cold the air is
(measured in degrees Celsius, °C,
or degrees Fahrenheit, °F)
CLIMATE is the average weather
a place gets over a long
period of time.

What is snow?

Snow is made up ice **crystals** that form from **water vapor** high in the **atmosphere**.

HOW DOES SNOW FORM?

As air gets warmer, it rises, and cools. Water vapor in the air **condenses**, or changes into droplets of liquid water. High in the atmosphere, it is so cold that the water droplets freeze into tiny ice crystals in the clouds. More ice forms around these, forming larger crystals, or snowflakes. As these fall through the air, they partly melt and collide with each other, forming fluffy lumps of snow.

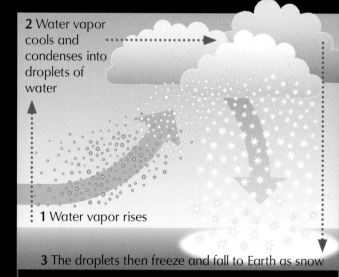

2 Water vapor cools and condenses into droplets of water

1 Water vapor rises

3 The droplets then freeze and fall to Earth as snow

▲ Tiny ice crystals form in the clouds. More ice forms around these, making snowflakes, which fall to the ground. If these fall through warm air, they melt and become rain.

▼ A blizzard in New York City. In heavy snow, getting around is almost impossible.

WHAT CAUSES SNOW AND BLIZZARDS?

When cold winds force warm air full of water vapor upward very fast, huge quantities of snowflakes form. These fall through the extremely cold air beneath them without melting, as dry, powdery snow. At the same time, the meeting of cold and warm air creates strong winds. The result is a combination of heavy snow and wind, called a blizzard. Even when the snow reaches the ground, it may be whipped up again, filling the air with snow.

SNOWFLAKES

There are several kinds of snowflake, depending on the conditions in the clouds where they form. Some are simple, six-sided forms, while others are more like tiny needles. The best-known are **dendrites**, which look like six-sided stars, flowers, or ferns. Others are small grains of ice, like frozen drizzle. Yet others are extremely small, six-sided plates that are found in the very cold north and south polar regions. They sometimes just hang in the atmosphere. They glitter in the sunshine, and are often called "diamond dust."

▼ Dendrites are six-sided crystals of ice. No two are ever exactly the same.

THE SNOWFLAKE MAN

Much of what we know about snowflakes was discovered by a Vermont farmer named Wilson Bentley (1865–1931). With little education, he became an expert on snowflakes. He photographed thousands of them, using a microscope and a camera. He discovered that no two snowflakes are ever exactly alike.

▼ Wilson Bentley became a world expert on the subject of snow and he developed a way of photographing magnified snowflakes. He obtained his first photographs of snowflakes in 1885.

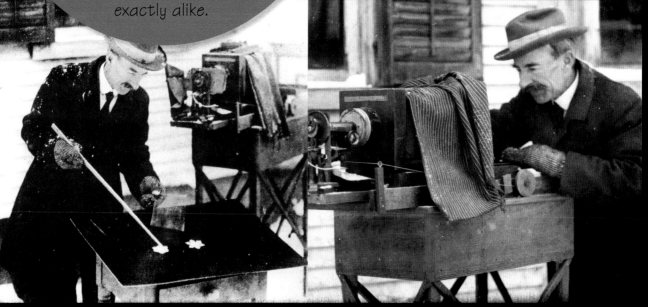

Where are blizzards most common?

Blizzards are common in parts of the world where warmer air full of moisture is most likely to meet very cold wind. These places are in the far north and south of the world, and at high **altitudes**—high above **sea level**.

ANTARCTIC BLIZZARD

Inland, in the **Antarctic**, there is rarely heavy snowfall, but there are blizzards. This is because the winds are extremely strong and cold. They blow the snow that lies permanently on the ground into the air, creating blizzard conditions.

▼ Young emperor penguins huddle together to protect themselves from an Antarctic blizzard.

PREVAILING WINDS

The winds that blow over the Earth's surface tend to travel in the same direction and are called prevailing winds. For example, just north and south of the **tropics**, the prevailing winds are "westerlies" (from the west). Westerlies are fairly warm and carry a lot of water vapor. Near the poles, the prevailing winds are cold easterlies (from the east). In winter, the easterlies are icy and strong. If the easterlies force themselves southward, they force the warmer air of the westerlies upward, creating snow and even stronger winds—perfect conditions for a blizzard.

▼ Cold easterly winds travel around the Earth near the North and South poles. If they force themselves southward, they meet warmer westerlies, creating blizzard conditions.

THE HEAVIEST SNOW

Certain parts of the world, such as the Great Plains and the Great Lakes in North America, often have severe snowfall and high winds in winter. Northwest Europe, parts of Russia, Korea, China, and Japan also often experience blizzard conditions. People there know the kinds of weather that will lead to a blizzard. For example, in Russia, when a cold wind called the "Buran" blows eastward from the **Arctic**, a blizzard is expected.

◄ Musk oxen live in the cold regions of Alaska, Canada, and Greenland. Their thick winter coat protects them from the coldest winter temperatures.

Mountain snow

The air at high altitudes is cooler than it is nearer to sea level. As a result, snow is common on the upper slopes of mountains and on high plateaux.

◄ A powerful avalanche races down the slopes of Mount Pumori, in the Himalayan range between Tibet and Nepal.

◄ These fences have been put up to help hold back avalanches in winter.

MOUNTAIN DANGERS

Blizzards are extremely dangerous on mountains. Climbers may suffer from the severe cold and, if they cannot see properly, they may slip and fall. Another great danger comes from avalanches. These are massive, fast-moving masses of snow that slide down mountainsides. They happen most easily when temperatures start to rise after heavy snowfall. The new snow becomes unstable. The slightest movement—a skier on the snow, or even a loud noise—can start an avalanche. Snow tears down the slope, carrying rocks and ice and burying everything in its path. Anyone on the mountainside may be swept to their death, and buildings at the foot of the mountain can be buried.

▲ Climbers tread carefully on mountain slopes. Where there is a danger that they may slip, they will rope themselves together.

THE SNOW LINE

The point on a mountain above which it is always snowy is called the **permanent snow line**. The altitude of this line varies according to where on Earth the mountain is, and the time of year. The warmer the sea-level temperature, the higher the snow line. Winds, temperature, and the amount of moisture in the air also affect the altitude of the snow line. The snow line on mountains in tropical regions can be as high as 18,700 feet, while in the Alps of Western Europe, it is about 6,500 ft (5,700 m) above sea level. The snow line is actually at sea level in polar lands.

▼ The permanent snow line is the lowest point on a mountain above which there is always snow.

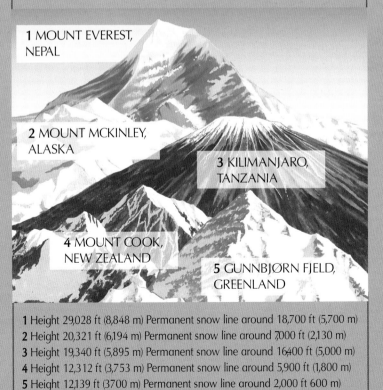

1 MOUNT EVEREST, NEPAL

2 MOUNT MCKINLEY, ALASKA

3 KILIMANJARO, TANZANIA

4 MOUNT COOK, NEW ZEALAND

5 GUNNBJØRN FJELD, GREENLAND

1 Height 29,028 ft (8,848 m) Permanent snow line around 18,700 ft (5,700 m)
2 Height 20,321 ft (6,194 m) Permanent snow line around 7,000 ft (2,130 m)
3 Height 19,340 ft (5,895 m) Permanent snow line around 16,400 ft (5,000 m)
4 Height 12,312 ft (3,753 m) Permanent snow line around 5,900 ft (1,800 m)
5 Height 12,139 ft (3700 m) Permanent snow line around 2,000 ft 600 m)

Getting around

Modern life can come to a standstill in a severe blizzard. High winds and heavy snowfall can bring down **power lines**, leaving whole communities without electricity. Travel may become impossible.

ROAD TRAVEL

Blizzards are extremely dangerous to anyone trying to make a journey on foot or in a car. It is easy to get lost in a **white out**—it is impossible to see anything because there is so much snow in the air. Driving is made even more difficult when high winds pile up snow into drifts, which can block roads completely. In countries where heavy snowfall is common, drivers prepare for snow by putting chains on their car wheels to stop them slipping on icy roads. They also carry shovels to clear drifts. However, the dangers of a blizzard are so great that people are usually warned not to go out at all.

▲ In countries where heavy snow is common, people often fix chains over their car tires to help them to grip icy surfaces.

▶ During a white out, it is difficult to see anything and people are advised not to drive because accidents are more likely.

▲ In December 2005, an aircraft skidded off the runway and onto a road in Chicago during a snowstorm.

RAIL, AIR, AND SEA

Railways can be blocked by drifting snow, and the cold temperatures may cause the points—the devices that trains use to change tracks —to become frozen and unusable. Strong winds and snow can make it impossible for aircraft to take off or land, and it is common for airports to be closed. At sea, crews on ships have difficulty seeing anything, while high winds can create huge waves. Freezing water on the upper parts of a small ship can make it top-heavy, causing it to capsize.

▶ Workers repair power lines during the 1998 **ice storm** in Canada.

ICE STORMS

When rain freezes as soon as it touches the ground, it is called an ice storm. In January 1998, one of the worst ice storms ever hit Canada and the northeast of the United States. More than 100,000 people left their homes to find warmth and safety. At least 25 people died, mainly from the cold.

Surviving a blizzard

People who live in places where blizzards are common need to know how to survive while they are cut off from the outside world.

▼ A snow hole is warmer and more comfortable than a tent, and provides better shelter during a blizzard.

STAYING SAFE OUTDOORS

Walkers and climbers should carry cell phones and, if possible, modern **navigation equipment**. Then, if they become trapped, they can tell rescuers where they are. Bright-colored **waterproof** clothing makes them easy to see. If snow is likely, they should not be outdoors but, if they are, it is a good idea to carry a shovel. Then they can dig a small shelter called a **snow hole** for protection until the storm is over and rescuers arrive.

▼ Cars can become completely buried in a snowdrift and have to be dug out.

INDOORS, OR IN A CAR

At home, it is important to stock up with food and drinking water. People need to be able to warm the house without gas or electricity, for example, by having plenty of firewood. Candles are useful, too. It is best to wear many layers of thin clothing to keep warm, and to wear something waterproof when going outside. Drivers who think there may be a risk should carry extra clothing, as well as blankets, food and drink, and a shovel. Anyone who is trapped should tie something brightly colored to the aerial and then stay inside their car.

SURVIVING IN THE SNOW

In 1943, during World War II, Norwegian Resistance fighter Jan Baalsrud fled from the Germans through the Arctic snow of northern Norway. He hid in a snow hole for more than a month before being rescued by local reindeer herders.

▲ Walkers in the snow should wear several layers of clothing to keep warm. These should be waterproof and brightly colored, so they can be easily seen during a rescue.

Dangers to health

Cold weather can bring a range of serious health problems. Even indoors, there can be dangers if people are trapped without proper heating and are cut off from sources of help and support.

SNOW AND WIND

One of the most serious problems that cold temperatures can bring is **hypothermia**. This is when the body temperature drops to dangerously low levels. If a person's body temperature drops to around 95°F (35°C), they may become dizzy and confused. At lower temperatures than that, they become unconscious and eventually die. Older people and babies are at special risk, but anyone trapped in a cold place can be in danger, especially if their clothing is wet. Low temperatures are made worse if there is a wind, as this cools body temperature much more than still air. This effect is called **wind chill**.

◄ In cold, snowy weather, ice can settle on the face, especially in hair. The face should be protected with a mask to avoid **frostbite**.

FROSTBITE

Extreme cold can cause frostbite—damage to the flesh that most commonly affects the face, fingers, and toes. It starts with the flesh going white and hard because the blood supply is withdrawn to save the body's heat. This causes the sufferer to feel a tingling sensation. The area affected becomes numb, and then red and swollen. Severe frostbite can damage the body so badly that the affected parts may have to be amputated, or removed.

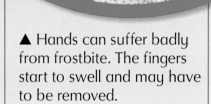

▲ Hands can suffer badly from frostbite. The fingers start to swell and may have to be removed.

TRAGEDY IN THE ANTARCTIC

In 1912, a team of British explorers, led by Captain Robert Falcon Scott, was caught in a blizzard on the way back from the South Pole. Captain Lawrence Oates had severe frostbite and knew he was slowing down the team, so he walked into the blizzard and was never seen again.

▶ Captain Robert Falcon Scott and his team of explorers died in 1912, as they returned from the South Pole.

Dealing with snow

Once a blizzard is over, the job of clearing up begins. In countries where heavy snowfall is common, this can be done quickly. If the blizzard is unusually severe, or if it happens where communities are not well prepared, clearing up can take many days.

CLEARING THE ROADS

Special machinery is used to clear roads. Snowploughs can push snow off roads, while snow blowers blow it from the surface, sometimes into a truck, to be taken away. In some countries, salt is spread on roads when snow is **forecast**. Salt brings down the freezing point of water, which helps to prevent ice from forming. Grit and sand can be spread on icy roads to stop tires slipping.

▶ A snowplough clears a road. In places where snow is common, these machines are kept on standby throughout winter.

► A **meteorologist** checks the depth of snow using an instrument called a **snow gauge**.

BE PREPARED

Accurate weather forecasts can save lives. If people know that a blizzard is on its way, they can stay indoors and stock up with food and fuel. Walkers and climbers can stay off the hills and mountains, and farmers can bring their animals in before the storms are at their worst.

▼ In parts of the world that often get heavy snowfall, people may have small snow blowers to clear pathways.

RESCUE SERVICES

After a heavy blizzard, people in isolated communities may be cut off from the outside world. Rescue organizations may have to drop food and medical supplies and airlift people to safety. Search and rescue teams once used dogs to try to find people trapped under heavy snow, and farmers still use dogs to find trapped livestock. Today, rescue helicopters can be fitted with **heat-sensitive cameras**, which can detect warm bodies trapped under the snow.

► When roads are blocked, the only way to reach someone who is sick or injured may be by helicopter.

Plants and animals

Plants and animals that naturally live in cold climates have developed a range of ways to live through harsh weather.

DRESSING FOR WINTER

In winter, the coat of many hunters, such as the Arctic fox, change to white, so they can hunt in the snow without being seen. Animals that are hunted, such as the Arctic hare, also have white coats to make them difficult to see.

HIBERNATION

Some animals avoid cold winters by **migrating** to somewhere warmer. A few creatures **hibernate**—they hide away and go into a very deep kind of sleep, when their body temperature drops and their heartbeat slows. Others, such as bears, get as fat as possible in fall, then find somewhere cozy to stay until warmer weather comes.

▲ Polar bear mothers spend winter in a den in the snow. Their cubs are born there and come outside in spring.

KEEPING WARM

Male Emperor penguins also build up stores of body fat, but they do not sleep. Instead, they spend the Antarctic winter looking after their eggs in temperatures as low as -40 degrees Fahrenheit, huddling together for warmth. In the Arctic, creatures such as musk oxen must live through the cold weather. They rely on thick fur to protect them from the cold, and know how to find grass beneath the snow. For lemmings and other small creatures, the snow provides shelter and they live safely underneath it. Farm animals, however, do not have the **adaptations** they need. Young animals are in danger of being buried in drifts, and can die from the cold and lack of food.

PLANT LIFE

The **cells** that make up a plant's stems or leaves can be damaged if they freeze. Some plants that grow in cold climates contain special chemicals that do not easily freeze. This allows the plants to live through very low temperatures. The pointed shape of fir and pine trees causes snow to slide off the branches, so they do not break under the weight of the snow.

▼ The branches of fir trees slope downward. This allows snow to slip off. If the branches were straight, they would break easily.

Living with snow

▲ The igloo is made from blocks of snow and is warm inside, even in the coldest winter weather.

IGLOOS

Some Inuit build traditional snow houses called **igloos**. Often, these are temporary homes, built quickly from blocks of snow and used during hunting trips. They provide shelter from extremely low temperatures and harsh, Arctic winter winds.

In some of the coldest parts of the world, people have known for centuries how to live through cold, snowy weather.

THE INUIT PEOPLE

Inuit is the name for several groups of people who traditionally live in the far north, close to the Arctic, in Canada, Alaska, Russia, and Greenland. Today, many Inuits live in modern houses, but some still follow the traditional way of life. They hunt and fish using spears and **harpoons**, travel on sleds drawn by husky dogs, and dress in reindeer furs.

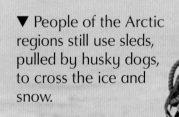

▼ People of the Arctic regions still use sleds, pulled by husky dogs, to cross the ice and snow.

▼ The **Sami** live in the far north of Scandinavia, where winters are harsh. The reindeer survive on a diet of lichens, which they find under the snow.

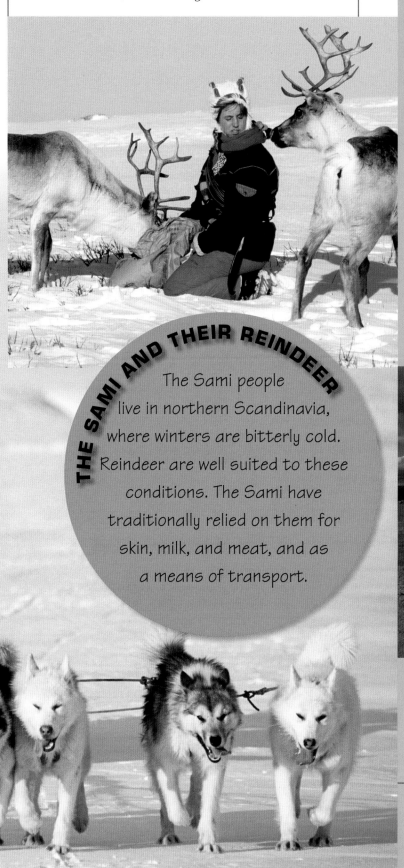

THE SAMI AND THEIR REINDEER

The Sami people live in northern Scandinavia, where winters are bitterly cold. Reindeer are well suited to these conditions. The Sami have traditionally relied on them for skin, milk, and meat, and as a means of transport.

THE ROOF OF THE WORLD

The country of Tibet lies among the mountains of Asia. This region is so high up that it is often called the "roof of the world." At this altitude, winters are harsh. Traditional houses are built with thick walls to keep out the cold. The kitchens and the cattle's stalls are on the ground floor. During the coldest months, the cattle are kept in these stalls and the heat from their bodies, as well as from the cooking stove, rises and warms the living space above.

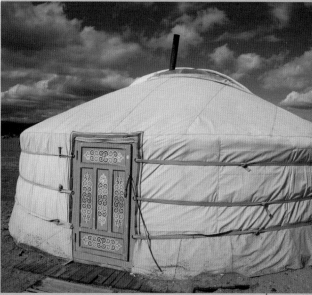

▲ A ger is the traditional felt tent used by the **nomads** of the high Mongolia plateau in Asia. Gers provide warm shelter, even in the cold winter.

Blizzard tales

Some blizzards are so severe, or do such great damage, that people remember them for many years.

THE GREAT SNOW

Four blizzards in New England between February and March 1717 became known as the Great Snow. There were drifts more than 24 ft (7.5 m) deep. It was said that people could step out onto snow from their first-floor windows. Thousands of cattle and sheep died. More recently, severe blizzards hit the United States in 1978—in Ohio and New England. Near the coast, the storm happened at the same time as high tides, bringing floods along with snow and causing around $500 million worth of damage in Massachusetts alone.

THE SNOW QUEEN

The children's story, The Snow Queen is by Hans Christian Andersen. It tells of a boy, Kay, who is taken by a magical Snow Queen during a blizzard to her ice palace in the far north. He is rescued through the love of a young girl, Gerda.

▲ The Snow Queen appears in a blizzard to a boy named Kay—and kidnaps him.

◀ A blizzard in 1978 struck the northeast of the United States, covering New York City in snow.

BRITAIN, 1947

In Britain, between January and March 1947, there was unusually heavy snow, with high winds. When it finally melted, there was also heavy rain and severe floods. The winter of 1962–1963 in Britain was actually much colder than 1947—it was the coldest for more than 200 years. However, it was not as snowy.

GENERAL WINTER DEFEATS NAPOLEON

Blizzards in Russia in the winter of 1812–1813 changed the course of history. A French invading army of several hundred thousand, led by Napoleon, reached Moscow, Russia, but was forced to retreat during a series of blizzards. Only around 10,000 soldiers made it back to France. The Russians said that Napoleon had been defeated by two great soldiers—General Starvation and General Winter.

▶ Soldiers of the French army trudge through the snow as they return from Moscow, Russia, in 1813.

▲ In 1947, the Royal Air Force prepared bread to be dropped to villages in Britain that were completely cut off due to heavy snow.

Coping with blizzards

No one can stop blizzards happening, but we can make sure our homes stay warm and safe, and there are modern ways to travel in snowy places.

▼ Crowds outside the Knickerbocker Theater, Washington D.C., in 1922. The snowstorm that brought its roof down became known as the "Knickerbocker Storm."

COLLAPSING ROOFS

In 1922, so much snow piled up on the roof of the Knickerbocker Theater, Washington D.C., that it fell in—killing 98 people and injuring 133. A similar accident happened in Poland in 2006, when the roof of a trade hall in Katowice collapsed, killing 66 people and injuring 150.

BUILDING FOR COLD WEATHER

Buildings can be built to last during cold weather and heavy snow. Sometimes, ideas developed in the past are still used. For example, houses in the Alps have always had steeply pitched roofs, allowing snow to slide off easily. Homes can be well insulated. Materials that work like thick blankets are put into the walls and under the roof to keep the warmth inside, and to keep the cold out. Windows can be double- or even triple-glazed, which means having two or three panes of glass in them. This helps to stop heat from escaping. In some countries, such as Canada, there are whole streets of shops built underground, away from harsh winter weather.

▲ Houses in the Alps have steep roofs, so that snow will not pile up.

KEEPING IN TOUCH IN THE SNOW

Isolated settlements can use radio communications to keep in touch with the outside world, even when power and telephone lines are down. Where heavy snow is common, people use sleds to get around, often pulled by dogs. They can also use **snowmobiles**—motor vehicles that travel on skis. There are even aircraft that can take off and land using skis.

◄ Snowmobiles can travel up to 50 miles (80 km) an hour. They are used both for travel and sport.

The changing climate

On average, temperatures around the world are getting warmer. Called **global warming**, it is causing changes in climate and could mean that extreme weather conditions happen more often.

PAST AND PRESENT

In the past, the Earth's climate has been both warmer and cooler than today. It is now getting warmer—very fast. Most scientists believe that humans are causing this. We are burning huge amounts of **fossil fuels**—coal, oil, and gas—creating **carbon dioxide** gas, which warms the Earth's atmosphere. Green plants absorb carbon dioxide, but we are destroying forests, which has made the situation worse.

▼ As the Earth's climate gets warmer, the ice in the seas around the Arctic and Antarctic will break up.

Sun's rays are reflected

Heat escapes

Sun's rays

Sun's rays are trapped, which warms the atmosphere

▲ The Sun warms the Earth and certain gases, such as carbon dioxide, trap some of the heat in the atmosphere. They act like the glass in a greenhouse.

THE FUTURE

Scientists report that winters in the Arctic and Antarctic have been warmer in recent years, and much of the ice that covers large areas of the land and sea has begun to melt. There is also less snow on some mountains, such as Kilimanjaro in Tanzania. No one really knows what weather patterns climate change will bring. Some places may get more extreme storms and blizzards, while regions that used to have snow regularly may no longer get any. However, scientists agree that, on average, temperatures over the world will continue to rise.

THE GREENHOUSE EFFECT

When the Sun heats the Earth's surface, this warms the air above it. **Greenhouse gases**, such as carbon dioxide, trap this heat. This is called the **greenhouse effect**— and causes the Earth to become warmer.

▲ Global warming does not always mean less snow. Record snowfall in New York in 2006 meant it was possible to ski in the city.

Glossary

ADAPTATION   A change to suit the environment or a way of life.

ALTITUDE   The height of a place above sea level.

ANTARCTIC   The region around the South Pole.

ARCTIC   The region around the North Pole.

ATMOSPHERE   The blanket of air around the Earth.

CARBON DIOXIDE   One of the gases in the air. Carbon dioxide is also produced when fuel is burned.

CELL   The smallest part of a living thing.

CONDENSE   To change from a gas into a liquid.

CRYSTAL   A clear, regularly-shaped solid.

DENDRITE   A branched crystal—six-sided snowflakes are called dendrites.

DRIFT   Snow heaped up by the wind.

FORECAST   To predict the future, such as the weather.

FOSSIL FUELS   Coal, oil, and natural gas. These fuels were formed millions of years ago from the remains of plants and marine animals.

FROSTBITE   The damage caused to parts of the body by exposure to severe cold.

GLOBAL WARMING   Increase in the average temperature of the air around the Earth. Global warming is caused by an increase in greenhouse gases, such as carbon dioxide, in the air.

GREENHOUSE EFFECT   The way that greenhouse gases trap warm air close to the Earth's surface.

GREENHOUSE GAS   One of the gases in the air that trap the Sun's heat. Greenhouse gases include water vapor, carbon dioxide, and methane.

HARPOON   A kind of spear with a rope tied to it, used for fishing and catching whales.

HEAT-SENSITIVE CAMERA   A camera that detects the amount of heat given off from objects and then shows this as pictures. Also called a thermograph.

HIBERNATE   A kind of sleep that is very close to death, when the body temperature drops and breathing and the heartbeat almost stop.

HYPOTHERMIA   When the body's temperature drops dangerously low.

ICE STORM   Freezing rain that covers everything with a layer of ice.

IGLOO   A traditional type of house made from snow by the Inuit people.

INUIT   A group of native people who traditionally live in the Arctic regions of the world.

METEOROLOGIST   A scientist who studies the weather.

MIGRATE   To move to another place. In animals, this means to travel from one place to another with the change in seasons.

NAVIGATION EQUIPMENT   Instruments used by ships and aircraft to help them to find out their position and route.

NOMAD   A wanderer. Some groups of people are traditionally "nomadic" because they spend their lives moving from place to place. For example, across grasslands or deserts, with their livestock.

PERMANENT SNOW LINE   The point on a mountain above which there is always snow.

PLATEAU   A flat area of high land.

POWER LINE   A heavy wire for carrying electricity.

SAMI   A group of people who traditionally live in northern Scandinavia, northern Europe.

SEA LEVEL   The level of the surface of the sea.

SNOW GAUGE   A scientific instrument for measuring how much snow has fallen.

SNOW HOLE   A cave dug out of the snow.

SNOWMOBILE   A motor vehicle with skis for traveling across the snow.

TROPICS   Part of the world on each side of the Equator between the Tropic of Cancer and the Tropic of Capricorn.

WATERPROOF   When water cannot pass through.

WATER VAPOR   Water in the form of a gas.

WHITE OUT   Snow in the air that is so thick, it is impossible to see through it.

WIND CHILL   The combined cooling effect of wind and cold temperatures.

FLOODS

What is a flood?

A flood occurs when a large amount of water covers land that is usually dry. Heavy rain and storms can cause flooding, **mudslides,** and **landslides**. Stormy weather can also whip up big waves that crash over the shore, covering the land in water.

▶ People in Villahermosa in Mexico had to flee their homes in October 2007 after floods swept the city.

WHY DOES FLOODING OCCUR?

When there is heavy rain, more water than usual flows into rivers, often causing the rivers to overflow. This is the most common cause of flooding and has a particularly disastrous effect if the river runs through a town or city. Lakes and even the ocean can overflow, too.

▼ **Meteorologists** try to predict the weather so that people can prepare for heavy rainfall and other extreme weather.

WHAT ARE THE EFFECTS OF A FLOOD?

Floods can ruin homes and destroy farm crops. In severe cases, people may drown. Flood water may cover buildings, wash away bridges and roads, and disrupt electricity and other supplies. Mud, garbage, and waste is washed everywhere. In towns and cities, waste water from streets and buildings drains into sewers. If there is too much water for the drains to hold, the dirty water flows back up the drains, so flood water is often contaminated with **sewage**.

▶ In June 2007, a freak storm flooded the village of Rotherham, England. People had to be rescued by dingy boat.

63

What causes rain?

Clouds are made of tiny droplets of water. When cooled, they can join together to make bigger drops. When the drops become too heavy, they fall to the ground as rain.

HEAVY RAIN

The heaviest downpours of rain come from huge black clouds called **cumulonimbus**. They form when warm, moist air rises quickly. The air tumbles around inside the cloud. This is called turbulence and makes the clouds look as though they are boiling. The turbulence pushes the water droplets around these huge clouds, causing them to crash into each other and form larger drops.

▲ Cumulonimbus clouds often form in summer. They are a sure sign of very heavy rain and perhaps a thunderstorm, too.

▼ A thunderstorm brings heavy rain to Johannesburg, South Africa.

THE WATER CYCLE

As the Sun heats the Earth, water from the surface of the oceans, lakes, and rivers **evaporates**—the water becomes a gas called water vapor and floats into the air. As the vapor rises, it cools and **condenses**—becomes water again—into tiny water droplets, which form clouds. The rain from these clouds falls on the land and soaks into the ground or runs into streams, rivers, and lakes. Most rivers flow into the ocean, where the water may evaporate and the cycle begins again.

Water vapor condenses to form clouds

Rain falls from clouds

Water evaporates into the air

Rainwater drains into rivers, lakes, oceans, and seas

▶ Water moves between the oceans, seas, air, and land in a continuous cycle called the water cycle.

HEAVY RAIN

Short bursts of heavy rain can happen almost anywhere in the world. On July 3, 1975, more than 16 in (40 cm) of rain fell in one hour in Shangdi, China.

Which places get the most rain?

It rains almost every day in some places on or near the **Equator**. Deserts, however, get almost no rain at all. The kind of weather a place usually gets is called its climate.

Tropic of Cancer

Equator

Tropic of Capricorn

▲ The **tropics** are the hottest places on Earth. They lie between the Tropic of Cancer and the Tropic of Capricorn.

▼ This village in southern Bangladesh was flooded when a **cyclone** hit the country in 2007.

WET CLIMATES

Places are often wet where the wind blows from the ocean onto the land. Winds bring rain from the Atlantic Ocean, for example, to the west coast of the British Isles. Some tropical areas are very wet. The heat of the Sun is strongest along the Equator, so more water evaporates from the ocean, creating heavy rain when the clouds blow over the land. **Monsoons** are winds that carry this rain over the land. They blow for part of the year, bringing a rainy season to some countries. In India, for example, the monsoon wind brings heavy rainfall from June to September.

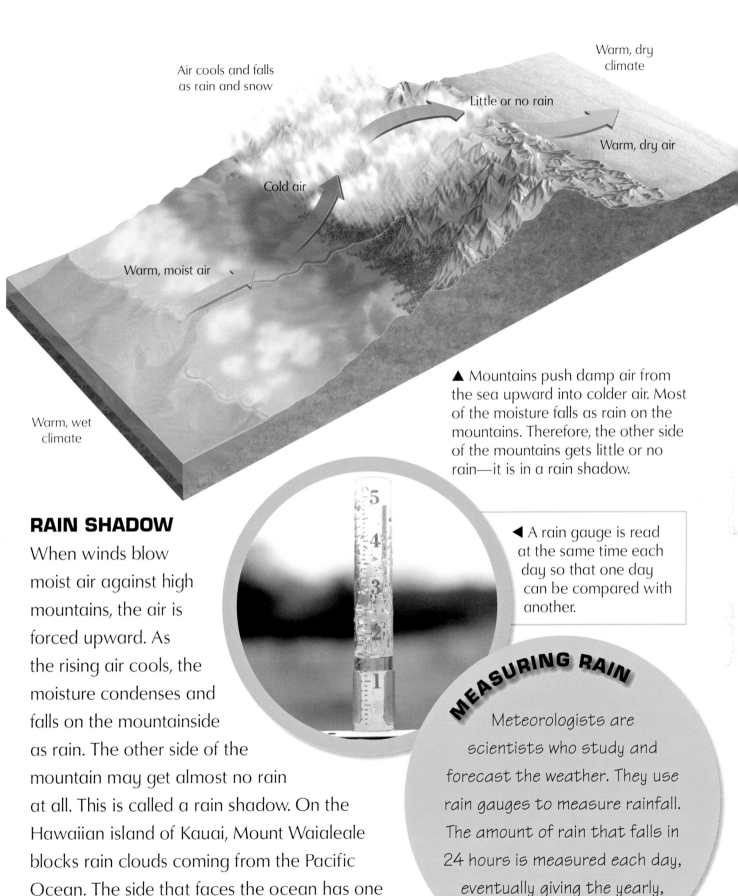

Air cools and falls
as rain and snow

Warm, dry
climate

Little or no rain

Cold air

Warm, dry air

Warm, moist air

Warm, wet
climate

▲ Mountains push damp air from
the sea upward into colder air. Most
of the moisture falls as rain on the
mountains. Therefore, the other side
of the mountains gets little or no
rain—it is in a rain shadow.

RAIN SHADOW

When winds blow
moist air against high
mountains, the air is
forced upward. As
the rising air cools, the
moisture condenses and
falls on the mountainside
as rain. The other side of the
mountain may get almost no rain
at all. This is called a rain shadow. On the
Hawaiian island of Kauai, Mount Waialeale
blocks rain clouds coming from the Pacific
Ocean. The side that faces the ocean has one
of the wettest climates in the world, with 460 in
(1,170 cm) of rain a year, but the other side is dry.

◄ A rain gauge is read
at the same time each
day so that one day
can be compared with
another.

MEASURING RAIN

Meteorologists are
scientists who study and
forecast the weather. They use
rain gauges to measure rainfall.
The amount of rain that falls in
24 hours is measured each day,
eventually giving the yearly,
or annual, rainfall.

Flooding rivers

River floods are usually caused by heavy rain. When rain falls for many weeks, the ground becomes so wet that rain cannot soak into it. The extra water drains into streams and rivers, which can cause them to overflow. Floods can also be caused by melting snow draining into rivers.

MISSISSIPPI-MISSOURI FLOOD

In 1993, heavy rain caused flooding along the Mississippi and Missouri Rivers. Towns were flooded and 10,000 homes were destroyed. In the city of St. Louis, where the rivers meet, some places remained underwater for 200 days. The flooding caused $20 billion worth of damage and is often called the Great Flood.

RISING WATER

A flood can take weeks to build up. The river water level rises and, in places, the water flows faster. Fast-flowing water creates a strong force that can wash away trees and bridges. Bridges are often built where the river is narrowest. The water can then become stuck and the level rises even more.

◀ People had to use canoes and other boats to go from house to house on land covered by the Mississippi-Missouri flood.

WHERE DO RIVERS FORM?

Rivers begin in mountains and hills.
Streams join together to make a
river, which then flows through the
valley into the sea. After heavy rain,
many rivers overflow their banks
onto the low-lying land beside the
river, called a **floodplain**.

When there is
too much extra water,
the floodplain cannot take
any more and nearby farmland,
towns, and cities are flooded.

▲ When the Severn River in England burst its banks in 2007, it flooded the surrounding land. The long line of trees shows where the river normally flows.

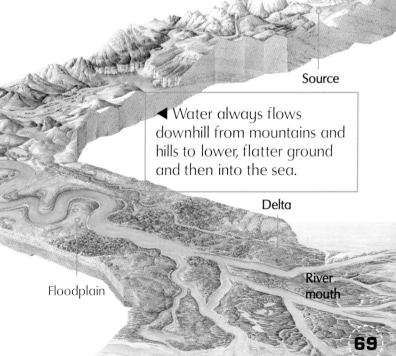

Source

◄ Water always flows downhill from mountains and hills to lower, flatter ground and then into the sea.

Delta

Floodplain

River mouth

Flash floods

Many floods take several days or weeks to build up, but flash floods can form in just a few hours. A heavy downpour of rain in one place quickly fills **gorges** and valleys. Some flash floods occur in deserts—the last place you might expect a flood.

▲ The streets became rivers in Boscastle in Cornwall, England, in the summer of 2004. Much of the damage was caused by trees and other debris that were swept along with the water.

VALLEYS

Flash floods are most likely to occur in summer, when the Sun's heat creates big thunderclouds. In August 2004, a seaside town of Boscastle, Cornwall, England, was hit by heavy rain that lasted several hours. The town is at the bottom of a steep valley. Water poured down the valley and through the town. It flooded homes and swept many cars into the harbor.

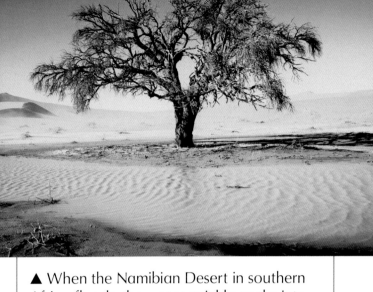

▲ When the Namibian Desert in southern Africa floods, the water quickly soaks into the ground.

▶ **Dams**, such as the Hoover Dam in Colorado, help to prevent floods by controlling the flow of water through them.

BURSTING DAMS

A dam is a wall built across a valley to block a river. It stores the water and often generates electricity, too. If the lake behind the dam becomes too full, the weight of water can burst the wall. Then billions of tons of water flood the area. In February 2005, the Shadikor Dam in Pakistan burst, killing at least 60 people and sweeping away five villages.

DESERTS

In a desert, flash floods usually begin with a thunderstorm and heavy rain. The ground is so dry and hard, the rainwater cannot soak in. Instead, it pours into **riverbeds** that are usually dry. The riverbed quickly becomes full of rushing water. Flash floods can begin in mountains far away, so they arrive without warning. The first sign may be the roar of the approaching wall of water, giving people little time to climb to safety on higher ground. Flash floods can hit cities, too. In August 2003, thunderstorms in the Southwest Desert produced heavy rain that flooded part of Las Vegas. Two people were killed and many motorists became trapped.

Mudslides

Heavy rain can cause landslides and mudslides on steep slopes. In a landslide, the water loosens part of the hillside so that rocks, trees, and boulders begin to slip downhill. In a mudslide, liquid mud pours down the slope.

CAUSES OF MUDSLIDES

Mudslides are most likely to occur on slopes where the trees have been cut down or burned in a **wildfire**. Tree roots hold the soil in place, so without them, the soil becomes loose and unstable. In heavy rain, the water mixes with the soil, which turns it into a liquid that can flow at speeds of up to 62 miles (100 km) an hour.

▶ In September 2002, this huge landslide blocked the Karmadon Gorge in Russia.

◀ Heavy rains in California in April 2006 caused a mudslide. Rescuers worked to free two people trapped in their home.

SUFFOCATING MUD

Landslides and mudslides block roads and trap people. Rescuing people can be difficult because the area is often hard to reach and the land is unstable. In October 2005, heavy rain from a **hurricane** triggered a mudslide that completely covered the village of Panabaj, Guatemala. In some places, the mud was 13 to 19 feet in depth. Rescuers used dogs to search for victims, but 400 people were never found.

▼ Search and rescue teams look for survivors after Guinsaugon, Leyte, was destroyed by a mudslide.

LEYTE, PHILIPPINES

In February 2006, a mudslide covered the mountain village of Guinsaugon on the island of Leyte in the Philippines. It is estimated that 200 people died and a further 1,500 people were never found.

Sea floods

Sometimes the sea floods the land. Storms create huge waves that crash onto the coast, but storms do the most damage at **high tide** because then the wind easily blows extra water onto the shore. Seawater can flood low-lying land, coastal towns, and villages.

TSUNAMIS

A tsunami can cause devastating sea floods. A tsunami is not caused by wild weather, however, but by an earthquake in the seabed. Huge waves hit the shore, flooding land along the coast.

▼ During a storm in November 2007, the sea wall in Lowestoft, England, was not high enough to hold back the waves at high tide.

HURRICANES

Hurricanes are tropical storms that begin over the ocean. They can create a **storm surge**—a bulge in the sea several feet high. This is higher than most shorelines. When the storm reaches land, the storm surge hits the coast and floods beyond the shore. High sea walls are built to keep out the waves. In August 2005, Hurricane Katrina hit New Orleans. Protective walls called **levees** collapsed and the storm surge swept into the city, flooding 80 percent of it.

▲ Many homes in New Orleans were almost completely covered by flood water following Hurricane Katrina.

LOW-LYING LAND

There is a higher risk of flooding for land that is not far above the level of the ocean. Bangladesh often floods during the rainy season because extra water in the Ganges River overflows onto the low-lying land. If a storm hits the coast, water floods onto the land from the river and the ocean. In some places, such as the Netherlands, the land is actually lower than the ocean. Here, the land has been **reclaimed** from the ocean. The water is held back by strong walls called **dykes**, and the low-lying land is built up, using soil and rocks, to a height that is less likely to flood.

▲ In the Netherlands, wind pumps help to keep the land drained of water.

Preparing for floods

Flash floods can happen without warning, but many floods can be predicted. River floods can build up over several days. Meteorologists track hurricanes and try to predict where they will hit land and how strong they will be.

▼ Sandbags are used to build a wall, keeping out flood water for a short time.

PREPARING FOR RIVER FLOODS

People who live close to rivers are most at risk of flooding. Local authorities use radio and television to warn people if they think a flood is likely. Sandbags are placed at the bottom of doorways to keep the water out, and valuable items are moved to higher floors. As the flood becomes more certain, electricity and gas supplies are turned off. Some people may have to leave their homes altogether and go to shelters that have been set up further away from the river.

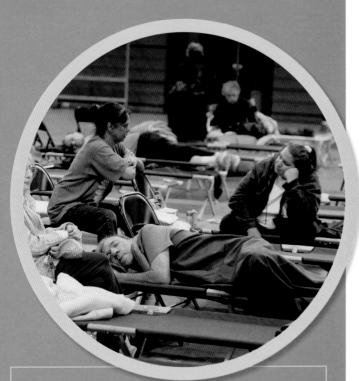

▲ In October 2005, a flood shelter was set up in Taunton, Massachusetts, when the authorities were worried that a nearby dam might burst.

EVACUATION

When a hurricane or river flood is expected, people who are likely to be badly affected get ready to leave their homes. People watch television or listen to the radio. When they are advised to evacuate their homes, they pack what they will need and travel inland or up to higher ground. Many people stay with friends or family. Other people go to flood shelters that the local authorities have organized, usually in schools, church halls, or sports stadiums. The shelters provide beds, blankets, and food until the flood is over.

▶ Filipino people walk to safety after their homes were flooded by a **typhoon**.

PREPARING FOR COASTAL FLOODS

It is difficult for meteorologists to predict exactly where a hurricane is likely to hit the coast. Many people prepare for the worst. They may buy in supplies of food and drinking water. As a hurricane gets nearer to a particular area, people are advised to leave the coast and move inland. **Evacuation** can take hours, as thousands of cars and other vehicles jam the roads.

Destructive power of water

Flood water can block roads, destroy bridges, and wash away cars and buildings. Even if people have been warned that there is risk of flooding, they may be taken by surprise. Flood water can rise quickly, trapping people in their homes or cars.

RESCUE OPERATIONS

Sandbags can keep water out, but only for a while. As the level rises, the water eventually seeps through. If the lower floor of a house fills with water, people have to go up to a higher floor. If the flood keeps rising, they may climb out onto the roof. In a town or village, rescuers may be able to reach stranded people by boat. If they cannot, helicopters lift people to safety.

▲ If flood water brings down a bridge, cars can be washed into the river.

◄ A helicopter rescues a woman from a building by the Limpopo River in Mozambique.

LARGE-SCALE FLOODING

If flooding covers a large area, millions of people can be affected. In November 2007, heavy rain flooded much of the state of Tabasco, Mexico. About 500,000 people were made homeless and millions were without electricity or clean water. When an electricity **power station** is flooded, the electricity supply can be cut for weeks. When electricity fails, water can no longer be pumped to towns and homes and, if the **water purification system** is flooded, the water supply has to be stopped.

WILDLIFE

Animals are also affected by floods. Where possible, farm animals are taken to higher ground, but wild animals have to look after themselves. Unless they can swim or get to higher ground in time, many smaller animals drown.

◄ In 2007, flood water surrounded the town of Tewkesbury, England, turning it into an island.

Repairing the damage

Once flood water has drained away, the repair work can begin—on damaged roads and bridges, and cleaning up buildings. Fire crews pump water out of basements, cellars, and other places where it may be trapped.

COST OF FLOODS
Hurricane Katrina hit in 2005 and was the most costly natural disaster ever, causing $125 billion worth of damage. Some damage was caused by the hurricane, but most was caused by flooding.

▼ During a flood, roads can be damaged and washed away.

INSIDE HOMES

Even shallow water can cause damage in a home. Flood water is dirty and often contaminated with sewage. Everything it covers becomes filthy. Carpets, floorboards, and walls become soaked. Wooden doors and cupboards bend when they are very wet, which means that they no longer shut. Water can make metal rust or corrode, ruining plugs and sockets. Gas pipes can also be damaged by flooding. Before work can start, the house has to be checked by experts to make sure it is safe.

▲ When flood water drains away, it leaves behind a layer of filth.

▼ Fire crews not only help to rescue people during a flood, they pump out water from flooded places.

CLEANING UP

When people return after a flood, they often find their homes have been ruined. Most of the furniture, carpets, and electrical goods that have been covered by water have to be thrown away. Electrical goods, such as televisions, refrigerators, and washing machines, that have been underwater no longer work. Machines called dehumidifiers are used to dry the walls, floors, and ceilings, but it can take months, sometimes years, before a building is completely dry and ready to be lived in again. Three years after Hurricane Katrina flooded New Orleans many people were still unable to return to their homes.

Preventing floods

One way to prevent floods is to build barriers to stop river water and the ocean from flooding the land. Another is to preserve trees and natural marshes, which soak up extra water. However, it is best not to build on land that is likely to flood.

FLOOD BARRIERS

The easiest way to stop a river flooding is to build a levee, which makes the riverbank higher. However, if the levee holds, it may just move the flood further downstream. Another way is to build an overflow ditch, called a **culvert**, alongside the river. After the 2004 flood in Boscastle, Cornwall, England, a culvert was built. When heavy rain hit the town again in 2007, flood water was diverted into the culvert and the town was saved from severe damage.

NATURAL WETLAND

Water meadows are grassy fields alongside riverbanks. Salt marshes and mangrove swamps are wetlands alongside the coast. They act like natural sponges soaking up and storing extra water. One reason that floods have increased in many countries is that many wetlands have been drained and new homes built on them.

▼ The Thames Barrier in London, England, stops seawater coming up the river when the tide is extra high or when wind pushes extra water inland.

▲ Water meadows regularly flood with water when the river is full.

DEFORESTATION

Many forests are being cut down, either to sell the wood or make farmland. Trees take up large amounts of water through their roots and are particularly important on mountainsides and hillsides. When trees are cut down, the water runs downhill into the rivers, making mudslides and floods more likely.

▼ Wildfires have destroyed all the trees on this hillside, making a mudslide more likely.

Living with floods

Today, many people are living in areas that are likely to flood. Some architects are beginning to design and build new homes that can survive a flood, but these houses are expensive.

▲ Rice is grown on **terraces** cut into the hillsides in Bali, Indonesia. The terraces catch the water and spread it evenly down the hill.

TAKING ADVANTAGE OF FLOODS

Rice needs plenty of water to grow, so many rice farmers plant their crops on flooded land called paddy fields. Tambaqui fish live in rivers in the Amazon rain forest, which regularly flood onto surrounding land. Then the fish swim among the trees to feed on fruit that has fallen into the water.

▼ Houses on the River Maas in the Netherlands look ordinary, but when the river rises, they rise with it.

KEEPING ABOVE THE WATER

For many years, people have built homes above the water or lived in floating homes, such as houseboats. In South East Asia, many traditional homes are built on **stilts**. In Lewes, England, one architect has started building modern homes on stilts. In the Netherlands, floating houses are becoming more common. The "basement" is full of air so that the house can float and the house is attached to two fixed poles. As the water rises, the house slides up the poles so it does not float away!

▶ Houses are kept out of the water with stilts. The stilts are strong enough to withstand the force of the water.

FLOOD-PROOFING

Ordinary houses can be adapted to make flooding less damaging. **Flood guards** keep out water better than sandbags because they have rubber seals to keep the water out for longer. Inside the building, tiled floors take the place of fitted carpets. Walls can also be made waterproof. Electric sockets are placed high up the walls, out of reach of shallow water, and washing machines and other electrical goods are placed on platforms above floor level. To stop sewage coming back into the house, special plugs can be pushed into the **U-bends** of waste pipes.

Are floods getting worse?

Climates around the world are changing. In the last 20 years, many places have suffered more extreme weather. The main reason for this is that the average temperature of the air is becoming warmer. This is called **global warming**.

GLOBAL WARMING

The Sun's heat is trapped in the Earth's atmosphere by **greenhouse gases**, including **carbon dioxide**. When **fossil fuels**—oil, coal, and natural gas—are burned, they produce carbon dioxide, which escapes into the air. In the last 50 years, people have been burning more and more fossil fuels.

DISAPPEARING ISLANDS

Some islands in the Pacific and Indian oceans are in danger of disappearing. Much of the land on the Maldive Islands is no more than 5 feet above sea level. Many people have already abandoned their homes because of frequent storms and floods.

Sun's rays are reflected

Heat escapes

Sun's rays

Sun's rays are trapped, which warms the atmosphere

▲ The Sun warms the Earth and certain gases, such as carbon dioxide, trap some of the heat in the atmosphere. They act like the glass in a greenhouse.

RISING SEA LEVELS

The level of the ocean is rising. Rising temperatures are melting **glaciers** and polar ice caps, pouring extra water into the oceans. As the air becomes warmer, the ocean below it warms up, too.

The warmer the oceans become, the more the water will expand, pushing up the level of the surface even more. Even a small increase in the level of the ocean causes flooding along low-lying coasts.

▼ Glaciers are slow-moving rivers of ice. They melt in the summer sunshine. The warmer the air becomes, the faster the glaciers melt.

Glossary

CARBON DIOXIDE One of the gases in the air. Carbon dioxide is also produced when fuel is burned.

CLOUD A floating mass of water droplets or ice crystals.

CONDENSE To change from a gas into a liquid.

CULVERT A drain or channel for water. A culvert alongside a river fills when the river floods.

CUMULONIMBUS A towering, dark cloud that often leads to heavy rain, thunderstorms, and hail.

CYCLONE A revolving tropical storm, also called a hurricane and a typhoon.

DAM A strong wall built across a valley to block a river or stream.

DELTA A triangular area of land and water at the mouth of a river. The land is formed by earth and sand washed down by the river.

DYKE A high bank built to stop the sea flooding onto land.

EQUATOR An imaginary line around the middle of the Earth, halfway between the North and South poles.

EVACUATION Organized removal of people from a dangerous building or area.

EVAPORATE To change from a liquid into a gas.

FLOOD GUARD A rubber seal that is fitted over doors and air vents to keep out flood water.

FLOODPLAIN Low, flat land alongside a river and onto which a river may often flood.

FOSSIL FUELS Coal, oil, and natural gas. These fuels were formed millions of years ago from the remains of plants and marine animals.

GLACIER A large, slow-moving river of ice.

GLOBAL WARMING Increase in the average temperature of the air around the Earth. Global warming is caused by an increase in greenhouse gases, such as carbon dioxide, in the air.

GORGE A steep, narrow valley, often with a stream or river running through it.

GREENHOUSE GAS One of the gases in the air that trap the Sun's heat. Greenhouse gases include water vapor, carbon dioxide, and methane.

HIGH TIDE When the sea comes highest up the shore. There are usually two high tides each day at any place on the coast.

HURRICANE A violent storm with strong winds and heavy rain that begins in the Atlantic Ocean or northeast Pacific Ocean.

LANDSLIDE A large amount of soil, rocks, and plants that slides down the side of a steep slope.

LEVEE A bank built to stop a river overflowing.

METEOROLOGIST A scientist who studies the weather.

MONSOON Wind in the tropics that brings weeks of heavy rain.

MUDSLIDE Mud mixed with water that flows downhill.

POWER STATION A building in which electricity is generated.

RECLAIMED Recovered or returned to a state in which it can be used.

RIVERBED A channel in the ground through which a river flows.

RIVER MOUTH The end of a river, where it flows into a lake or the sea.

SALT MARSH Marshy ground, often covered by salt water from the ocean.

SEWAGE Waste material and water from toilets and drains.

SOURCE The place from which something comes. The source of a river is the place where it begins, usually on a hill or mountainside.

STILTS Poles that raise a building above the ground.

STORM SURGE A rapid rise in the level of the sea caused by storm winds blowing towards the shore.

TERRACES Wide, flat steps cut into a hillside to give land for growing plants.

TROPICS Part of the world on each side of the Equator between the Tropic of Cancer and the Tropic of Capricorn.

TYPHOON A tropical storm that begins in the northwest Pacific Ocean and moves west, hitting countries from the Philippines to Japan.

U-BEND U-shaped bend in a waste pipe that traps a small amount of water and stops smells coming back up the pipe.

WATER MEADOW Flat, grassy land beside a stream or river that is flooded from time to time.

WATER PURIFICATION SYSTEM A way of cleaning water to make it safe to drink.

WETLAND Land, such as a swamp or marsh, that is wet most of the time.

WILDFIRE Fire in the countryside that is hard to put out.

HURRICANES and TORNADOES

Hurricanes and tornadoes

Hurricanes and tornadoes are dangerous weather that can kill people and animals, and damage farm **crops**, buildings, and other property. Tornadoes whip up the strongest winds on Earth.

▶ An anemometer is an instrument that measures the speed of the wind.

HURRICANES

A hurricane is a huge storm with violent winds that develops over the ocean. Winds of more than 75 miles (120 km) an hour and heavy rain clouds swirl around the center of the hurricane, which is called the "**eye.**" The eye is an area of stillness and calm. The storm, which can be hundreds of miles wide, moves across the ocean. A hurricane becomes stronger as it travels over warmer water toward the coast. When a hurricane hits land, it quickly loses its strength because the ocean provides it with the energy and moisture it needs to exist. A hurricane wreaks damage across a wide area, causing the most destruction on islands and in coastal areas.

WEATHER AND CLIMATE

WEATHER is...
wind—movement of the air
visibility—how far we can see in the air
precipitation—rain, snow, or hail
temperature—how hot or cold the air is
(measured in degrees Celsius, °C,
or degrees Fahrenheit, °F)
CLIMATE is the average weather
a place gets over a long
period of time.

TORNADOES

A tornado is a storm with violently rotating wind. It looks like **funnel**-shaped cloud. A tornado usually develops under a big **thundercloud**. It does not last long but its winds are often much faster and stronger than those of a hurricane—they can reach 300 miles (500 km) an hour. The biggest tornadoes are 1 mile wide, but most are less than 1,600 ft (1.5 km) wide. A tornado can destroy everything in its narrow path.

▲ A tornado forms as a thin funnel under a heavy thundercloud.

▼ Hurricane Andrew hit Miami in Florida, on August 23, 1992.

What is wind?

Wind is air moving across the surface of the Earth, as a gentle breeze or a strong wind. Wind is caused by the Sun heating some parts of the Earth more than others. As the ground warms up, it heats the air above. The warm air then rises and cooler air rushes in. The faster the warm air rises, the faster cooler air moves in and so the stronger the wind.

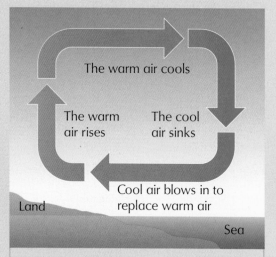

The warm air cools

The warm air rises

The cool air sinks

Cool air blows in to replace warm air

Land

Sea

▲ Warm air rises, pulling in cooler air to take its place. The rising air cools and falls back toward the Earth's surface.

▼ The main prevailing winds blow toward the Equator, and toward the North and South poles.

RECORD WIND

The highest wind speed ever recorded is 231 miles (372 km) an hour, on Mount Washington in 1934. The worst tornadoes may produce winds of 310 miles (500 km) an hour, but their speeds have never been accurately measured.

PREVAILING WINDS

In most places, the wind blows from one direction most of the time. This is called a **prevailing wind** and it varies in different parts of the world. For example, in the tropics, prevailing winds blow toward the **Equator**. The Sun's rays are strongest over the Equator and so as hot air rises, cooler air from the north and south is pulled in. The cooler air forms the prevailing winds.

BEAUFORT SCALE

STRENGTH	WIND SPEED	EFFECT
0 Calm	0 mi (0 km) an hour	Chimney smoke rises straight up
1 Light air	0.5–3 mi (1–5 km) an hour	Smoke drifts gently
2 Light breeze	3.5–7 mi (6–11 km) an hour	Leaves rustle, wind felt on face
3 Gentle breeze	7.5–12 mi (12–19 km) an hour	Leaves and twigs on trees move
4 Moderate breeze	12.5–18 mi (20–29) an hour	Small branches move
5 Fresh breeze	18.5–24.5 mi (30–39 km) an hour	Small trees start to sway
6 Strong breeze	25–30 mi (40–50 km) an hour	Large branches move
7 Near gale	31–38 mi (51–61) an hour	Whole trees sway
8 Gale	38.5–46 mi (62–74 km) an hour	Twigs broken off trees
9 Severe gale	46.5–54 mi (75–87 km) an hour	Small branches and tiles blown off
10 Storm	54.5–63 mi (88–102 km) an hour	Houses damaged, trees blown down
11 Severe storm	64–74.5 mi (103–120 km) an hour	Serious damage
12 Hurricane	74.5 mi (120 km) an hour+	Widespread damage

LOCAL WINDS

Winds are affected by the landscape. High mountainsides get more wind than low-lying land in **valleys**. Similarly, places along the coast or beside large lakes are often windy. Land warms up and cools down faster than water. During the day, when the land becomes much warmer than the sea, the wind blows from the sea to the land. The opposite happens at night—the land is cooler than the sea, so the wind blows from the land to the sea. The force of the wind is measured by the **Beaufort scale**.

▶ It is easy to see which way the prevailing wind blows on this hillside—the trees have grown away from the wind.

Where do severe storms occur?

Hurricanes and tornadoes can happen in most parts of the world, but they are most frequent in particular places at particular times of the year. Hurricanes usually start as **tropical** storms, which form over warm water near the Equator. They are pushed hundreds of miles across the sea by prevailing winds. Tornadoes form below severe thunderstorms.

▼ Severe storms are called hurricanes, **typhoons**, and **cyclones** in different parts of the world.

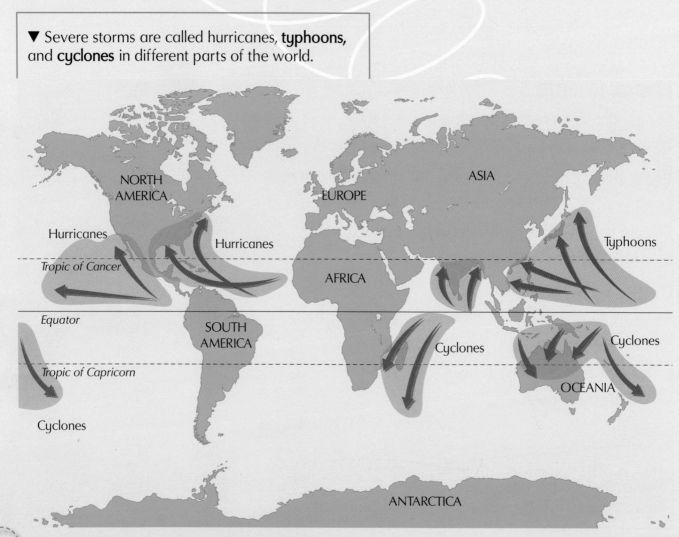

TROPICAL STORMS

Hurricane, typhoon, and cyclone are different names for severe tropical storms. Hurricanes form over the Atlantic Ocean and move toward the Caribbean Sea and the Gulf of Mexico. They occur between May and October. Storms that form in the eastern Pacific Ocean, north of the Equator, are also called hurricanes. Typhoons form in the northwest Pacific Ocean and are most frequent in summer. They strike countries from the Philippines to Japan. Cyclones form in the southern Pacific Ocean and Indian Ocean. They hit countries from Bangladesh, in the northern Indian Ocean, to Mozambique in east Africa, and Australia.

▶ Many houses in Qianzhang village in southeastern China were destroyed by Typhoon Saomai in August 2006. It was the worst typhoon for 50 years.

▼ Meteorologists watch a large thunderstorm in Tornado Alley to see if a tornado will develop below it.

TORNADO ALLEY

Tornadoes can form almost anywhere, but the United States gets more tornadoes than anywhere else in the world— about 800 a year. Most of these are in "Tornado Alley," an area in the Great Plains region that stretches from the state of Texas to South Dakota. Australia gets the second most tornadoes each year, but Bangladesh, China, India, and England are hit frequently, too.

TYPHOON

In the past, people explained storms and wild weather through myths and the gods. In Greece, Typhoon was a gigantic monster with 100 heads, who terrified the gods. He was killed by Zeus but his sons, the storm winds, survived.

How does a hurricane form?

A hurricane begins over an ocean, about 30 to 60 miles (50 to 100 km) north or south of the Equator. It forms when a tropical storm moves over an area of rising warm, moist air. The storm becomes stronger, causing winds to spiral faster around its center.

SWIRLING WINDS

A hurricane forms above the ocean where the temperature of the sea is more than 80°F (27°C). Water evaporates and the warm, moist air quickly expands and rises. This pulls in strong winds of cooler air underneath. The spin of the Earth causes the winds to rotate. North of the Equator, the winds spin counterclockwise and south of the Equator, they move clockwise. The winds spin around the center, called the eye. The strongest winds are closest to the eye, in the **eyewall**.

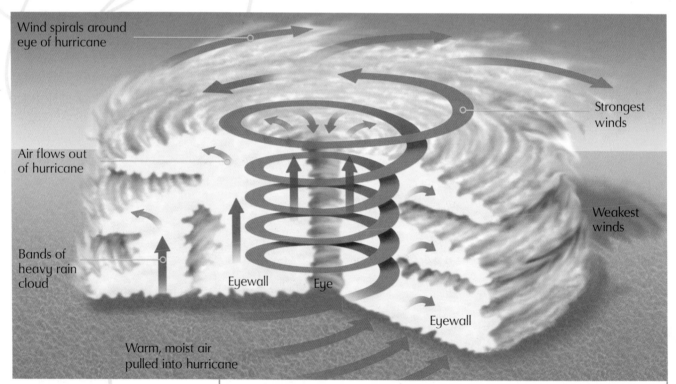

Wind spirals around eye of hurricane

Strongest winds

Air flows out of hurricane

Weakest winds

Bands of heavy rain cloud

Eyewall

Eye

Eyewall

Warm, moist air pulled into hurricane

▲ A hurricane consists of a huge spiral of strong winds and rain. The eye at the center of the hurricane is an area of calm.

▲ A hurricane hunter flies into the eye of a hurricane to photograph the eyewall.

TRACKING A HURRICANE

Some hurricanes disappear before they reach land. Others become stronger as they move over warmer water. In the Atlantic Ocean and northern Pacific Ocean, the strength of a hurricane is rated according to the **Saffir-Simpson scale.** Scientists called meteorologists use weather balloons, **radar,** and weather satellites to look for new hurricanes. Hurricane hunters are special aircraft that fly right into the eye of a hurricane to measure its strength. Photos taken by weather satellites help meteorologists to track its route.

► A photograph of Hurricane Katrina taken by a **weather satellite** on August 29, 2005, just as the hurricane hit New Orleans.

SAFFIR-SIMPSON SCALE

STRENGTH	WIND SPEED	DAMAGE
1 Weak	73–95 mi (119–153 km) an hour	Some damage to signs an trailers
2 Moderate	55.6–109 mi (154–177 km) an hour	Considerable damage to trailers, some damage to roofs and trees
3 Strong	110–129 mi (178–209 km) an hour	Large trees blown over, trailers destroyed, damage to buildings, flooding
4 Very strong	130–154 mi (210–249 km) an hour	Much damage to buildings, roofs blown off
5 Devastating	154 mi (249 km) an hour+	Severe damage to buildings, small buildings blown away, coastal flooding

Preparing for a hurricane

A hurricane takes several days to develop and move across the ocean before it reaches land. This gives meteorologists time to warn people who live in its path. However, a hurricane can change its direction, or course, at any time, so it is difficult to predict exactly where it will strike the coast.

NAMING HURRICANES

Hurricanes are given names. The first hurricane of the season is given a name beginning with A, the second with B, and so on. The first six names for hurricanes in the Atlantic Ocean in 2010 are Alex, Bonnie, Colin, Danielle, Earl, and Fiona.

HURRICANE WARNING

Most countries have a system of hurricane warnings. In the United States, a hurricane warning means that a hurricane is likely in the next 24 hours. People listen to their radios and television for the most up-to-date news. They bring in porch furniture and other loose things that are outside. Offices, schools, and other organizations stop work so people can go home.

▲ These people were still on the street when Hurricane Katrina hit Florida. They are in serious danger of being blown away or hit by flying **debris**.

STORM APPROACHING

As the storm gets nearer, people pull shutters down over their windows or cover them with wood to stop the glass being broken by the wind. If their homes are strongly built and unlikely to **flood**, some people may decide to stay there during the storm. If so, they have to keep away from windows and doors connecting to the outside. In many areas, however, people will be told to **evacuate**, or leave, their homes. They have to move to somewhere safer inland. Then they pack essential things and join the long lines of traffic leaving the coast.

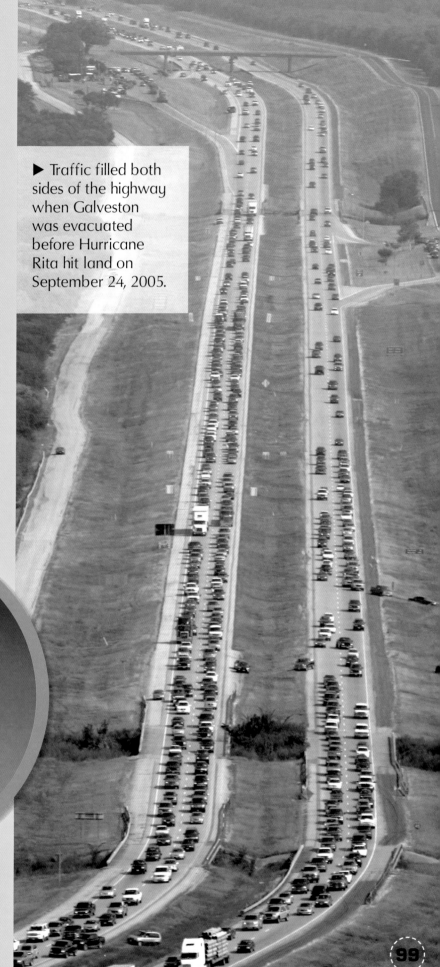

▶ Traffic filled both sides of the highway when Galveston was evacuated before Hurricane Rita hit land on September 24, 2005.

▲ Covering windows with wood stops them being broken during a hurricane.

Destructive power

Hurricanes bring three forces of destruction—strong winds, heavy rain, and high seas. As the storm approaches, the wind becomes stronger and the rains heavier. When the eye of the storm passes over, the wind and rain stop completely.

HURRICANE KATRINA

In 2005, Hurricane Katrina caused flooding in New Orleans. Water from the heavy rain and storm surge piled up in nearby Lake Ponchartrain until it burst through the **levees**. Water flooded 80 percent of the city, killing more than 1,800 people and causing $96 million worth of damage.

▲ Water flooded the streets of New Orleans after Hurricane Katrina hit the city on August 29, 2005.

WIND AND RAIN

Hurricanes are rated according to their strength. Trees, trailers, and cars are easily damaged by wind. Shop signs, garbage cans, and anything that is not securely fixed may be tossed about by the wind. Trees bend and their branches break off. In the strongest hurricanes, whole trees are uprooted, roofs are blown off houses, and, unless they are strongly built, whole houses are blown over. Heavy rain fills rivers and drains, which can overflow and cause flooding. The worst flooding in a hurricane is caused by the sea.

STORM SURGE

The rising air around the center of a hurricane makes the sea below it bulge upward. When it blows toward the land, the bulge can be more than 20 ft (6 m) in height. This is called a **storm surge**. When the hurricane hits the coast, the storm surge raises the level of the sea. The strong winds whip up giant waves that crash onto the shore. Unless the coast has good **flood defences**, the waves flood the land. They can push boats far inland and wash cars and debris into the sea.

▼ Massive waves battered the coast of Cuba during Hurricane Rita in September 2005.

▲ In May 2008, Cyclone Nargis swept through Burma, killing thousands of people and destroying villages and towns. Here families on Haing Guy Island are trying to dry out what remains of their possessions.

Thunderstorms

Hurricanes often include thunderstorms, and most tornadoes form below thunderclouds. Even on their own, thunderstorms can be very destructive. A flash of **lightning** contains a huge charge of electricity with a temperature that can be hotter than the surface of the Sun!

HOW DOES A THUNDERSTORM FORM?

Thunderstorms form where warm, moist air is rising rapidly, usually in summer. The air contains large amounts of **water vapor.** As it rises, the water vapor cools and **condenses** to form a black cloud of water droplets. The air in the cloud is still warmer than the air around it, however, so it continues to rise, carrying the water droplets with it. Some of the moisture in the air freezes to form ice crystals. Strong winds push the water droplets and ice around the cloud.

▼ These hailstones are as large as eggs. They fell on Kansas.

HAIL

Thunderstorms often bring hail. As ice crystals move around inside the thundercloud, layers of ice freeze around them, forming hailstones. They fall to the ground when they become too heavy to stay in the cloud.

▼ A flash of lightning rips through the sky. It only lasts for a few seconds and is followed by **thunder.**

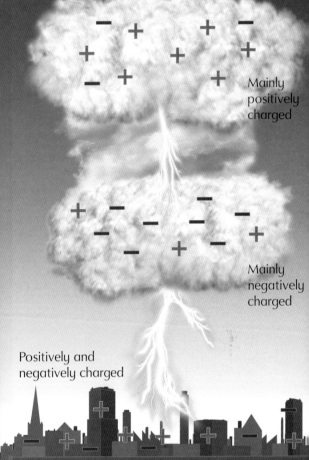

▼ Most lightning leaps from one part of a cloud to another, but some jumps from the cloud to the ground.

Mainly positively charged

Mainly negatively charged

Positively and negatively charged

LIGHTNING AND THUNDER

As the droplets of water and ice crystals are pushed violently around in the cloud they collide. They rub against each other and become electrically charged. The top of the cloud becomes positively charged and the bottom becomes negatively charged. This creates a giant spark, called lightning. Lightning lasts for less than a second, but it is so hot it makes the air around it suddenly expand. Thunder is the sound of the air being blasted apart.

How does a tornado form?

A tornado is a whirling funnel of air. It usually forms below a thundercloud, but it can also form after a hurricane strikes land. Tornadoes are the most violent type of weather, but usually they only last a few minutes.

▼ A tornado has just begun to form below this heavy black thundercloud.

FIRST SIGNS

The first sign of a tornado could be a green-colored sky, or light rain that becomes heavy and mixed with hail. A tornado can also form on a clear day with no thunderstorm or hail. The first sign may be dust swirling above the ground.

BIRTH AND DEATH OF A TORNADO

A thundercloud contains strong **updrafts** and **downdrafts**. The strongest tornadoes begin in **supercell thunderclouds**, which have an extremely strong updraft of up to 160 miles an hour. Before a thundercloud produces a tornado, the rising air begins to spin. It spins because wind near the top of the cloud is blowing at a different speed or in a different direction from the wind lower down in the cloud. The tornado first appears as a funnel below the cloud. It grows longer and reaches down toward the ground. As the tornado moves across the land, it loses energy. The funnel becomes thinner, the winds slow down, and the tornado shrinks back into the thundercloud.

▲ A tornado ends when the funnel shrinks back into the cloud. Clear sky follows behind the thunderstorm.

A CHAIN OF TORNADOES

Tornadoes often occur one after the other. A supercell thundercloud can produce six or more violent tornadoes. In April 1974, the United States experienced the worst outbreak of tornadoes ever. In just 16 hours, 148 tornadoes touched down over 13 states, from Alabama to West Virginia. These deadly twisters killed 330 people and caused major destruction across 2,500 miles (4,000 km) of land.

◄ A tornado at its height. It makes a deafening roar as it travels across the land.

Preparing for a tornado

When thunderclouds form, meteorologists try to assess whether the storm will produce a tornado. They track the storm and use radar to find out whether any of the clouds contain rotating, rising air. When they think a tornado could form, they issue a tornado warning.

UNPREDICTABLE

It is difficult for meteorologists to predict which thunderstorms will produce tornadoes. Even when a funnel has been spotted, it is difficult to work out the path of a tornado because it can change direction at any time.

▼ These meteorologists in Wichita, Kansas, are tracking thunderstorms and tornadoes in Tornado Alley.

▲ The safest place to be during a tornado is in an underground shelter.

TORNADO WARNING

When meteorologists think that tornadoes could form, they issue a tornado watch or c tornado warning. People listen for warning on radio and television. Some people have weather radios that only come on when there is a tornado warning. When a tornado watch is issued, people bring in any loose objects from outside. When a tornado warning is issued, they find shelter. Many buildings have storm shelters, usually below ground level. If they do not have a storm shelter, people go into an inside room o hallway away from windows and outside doors Motorists are told to leave their cars and shelter in a ditch. They should not try to escape by driving faster than the storm.

▼ Storm chasers use trucks packed with equipment, including radar, a computer, and radio.

STORM CHASERS

Instead of trying to avoid a tornado, **storm chasers** try to find them. Some storm chasers are tourists, but most are scientists who want to study tornadoes in detail. Storm chasers follow thunderstorms in special vehicles. The vehicles have radar, cameras, and other equipment to measure and record the tornado. Storm chasers may follow storms for weeks before they find a tornado. When they do, they try to get as close as possible without getting caught. This is a very dangerous job.

Destructive power of a tornado

Tornadoes are also called twisters because the wind spirals in such a tight circle. Most tornadoes are less than 1,500 ft (500 m) wide, although the strongest tornadoes may be nearly four times this width. A tornado's path of destruction is much narrower than other storms, but a tornado's strong winds can cause greater damage.

MEASURING TORNADOES

It is not possible to measure the wind speed of a tornado because it is over so quickly. Instead the **Fujita scale** rates a tornado and its wind speed from the damage it causes. The power of the wind increases faster than the speed. For example, a wind of 200 miles (320 km) an hour is four times, not twice, as powerful as a wind of 100 miles (160 km) an hour.

▼ The tornado that struck Greensburg in Kansas, on May 4, 2007 destroyed most of the town and was the worst tornado to hit the country for ten years.

PATH OF DESTRUCTION

Damage from a tornado is limited. The houses on one side of a street may be flattened, while houses on the other side are hardly affected. Cars and mobile homes are easily overturned. The rising column of air in the center of the tornado sucks up dust and litter, as well as heavier things, such as cars and even people— dropping them many feet away. The strongest tornadoes can last for up to an hour and travel at up to 60 miles (100 km) an hour.

◀ A tornado has sucked this huge tree out of the ground and smashed it into the house.

▶ This house in London, England, was ripped apart by a tornado in December 2006. The houses across the street were undamaged.

FUJITA SCALE

CATEGORY	ESTIMATED WIND SPEED	DAMAGE
0 Light	65–85 mi (105–137 km) an hour	Branches of trees broken
1 Moderate	86–109 mi (138–177 km) an hour	Roofs damaged, broken windows
2 Considerable	111–135 mi (178–217 km) an hour	Large trees blown over, roofs blown off, mobile homes destroyed
3 Severe	135.5–165 mi (218–266 km) an hour	House walls collapse, cars overturned
4 Devastating	165–200 mi (267–322 km) an hour	Houses totally destroyed, cars lifted
5 Incredible	200 mi (322 km) an hour +	Large buildings damaged, cars thrown more than 300 feet

Strange happenings

A **waterspout** is a tall column of rising air and water. It is a kind of tornado that forms over warm water in the sea or a lake, and moves across the surface. It can cause unusual events, including showers of fish or frogs.

▲ A waterspout in the Gulf of Mexico. Waterspouts usually last between ten and 30 minutes. Most waterspouts are less powerful than tornadoes.

WATERSPOUTS

A waterspout forms when warm, moist air rises quickly above an area of water. It starts as a whirling pattern on the surface of the water and becomes visible when the water vapor in the air condenses to form a column of water drops. As the waterspout becomes stronger, it sucks up water from the surface of the sea or lake. The winds that spin around a waterspout are much slower than around a tornado, probably because the weight of the water slows them down. A waterspout can overturn boats and, when it moves over land, it can become a weak tornado.

DUST DEVILS

A **dust devil** can arise quite suddenly, usually in a **desert**. There may not even be a thunderstorm or rain. A dust devil begins when the air just above the ground overheats. It rises and begins to swirl. The rising air sucks up dust and sand, which makes it easy to see as it travels across the land.

▲ This dust devil was photographed swirling across land in Potosí District, Bolivia.

RAINING FISH

A waterspout's rising column of air can suck up fish, frogs, and other things along with the water. The fish are lifted high into the air and blown along by the strong wind. They may travel for many miles before they eventually fall to the ground. On August 18, 2004, the village of Knighton, Wales, was hit by a shower of fish.

◄ Showers of fish and frogs have been reported in many countries around the world.

The aftermath

Hurricanes and tornadoes can leave behind devastated villages, towns, and cities. People may be killed and many more injured or reported missing. It can take years to clear up and repair the damage.

▼ Cyclone Larry struck North Queensland in Australia in March 2006. No one was killed, but it caused millions of dollars worth of damage.

DEADLIEST HURRICANES

In 1970, the Bhola Cyclone hit the Ganges River in eastern Pakistan (modern-day Bangladesh), killing 500,000 people—the highest number of deaths for a cyclone. The deadliest Atlantic hurricane struck the Caribbean in 1780, killing 22,000 people.

▼ Houses in New Orleans that were damaged by Hurricane Katrina are now being repaired. It will take many years before all the work is complete.

WIND DAMAGE

Strong winds lift off tiles or tear off whole roofs and blow down walls. Buildings may be so badly damaged that they are unsafe and have to be rebuilt. A tornado can flatten buildings completely. Strong winds also blow down trees and **power lines**, cutting the supply of electricity. Trees may block roads and railroads. Cars and mobile homes can be overturned and smashed. Buildings that are strongly built are most likely to survive a hurricane or tornado.

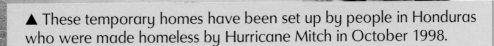
▲ These temporary homes have been set up by people in Honduras who were made homeless by Hurricane Mitch in October 1998.

FLOOD DAMAGE

Flood water is usually polluted with dirt and **sewage**, which makes cleaning up more difficult when the water eventually drains away. The storm surge of a hurricane brings the worst flooding. In Bangladesh in November 2007, flooding washed away thousands of villages. More than three million people were affected and millions of dollars were needed to feed and shelter people who had lost their homes.

Are hurricanes and tornadoes increasing?

In the last 20 years, severe hurricanes, floods, and droughts have been occurring more often. The most likely reason for this is that the average temperature of the air is increasing. This is called **global warming.**

WHAT CAUSES GLOBAL WARMING?

Global warming is caused by an increase of certain gases, including **carbon dioxide** and methane, in the air. They are called "greenhouse gases" because they trap the Sun's heat, like a giant greenhouse. People are increasing the amount of **greenhouse gases** in the air by burning oil, coal, and natural gas. Most cars, trucks, and airplanes burn oil in their engines, and most power stations burn coal, oil, or natural gas to produce electricity.

Sun's rays are reflected

Heat escapes

Sun's rays

Sun's rays are trapped, which warms the atmosphere

▲ The Sun warms the Earth and certain gases, such as carbon dioxide, trap some of the heat in the atmosphere. They act like the glass in a greenhouse.

WHAT WILL HAPPEN?

Scientists believe that, unless global warming is controlled, hurricanes, floods, and droughts will become even more common.

The oceans warm up very slowly, but even a small rise in the temperature of the sea makes it more likely that hurricanes will form and become more severe. Governments and people need to act fast. They need to find new ways of doing things that produce less greenhouse gases. Scientists are developing engines that burn hydrogen instead of oil. Power stations already exist that use the power of the Sun, flowing water, and even the wind to produce electricity. None of these produce carbon dioxide.

▲ This is what cars might look like in the future. The cleanest cars will run on hydrogen.

▼ Wind turbines produce electricity without producing greenhouse gases. They work best in windy places, such as out at sea, on open plains, or on the top of hills.

WIND TURBINES

The wind can be used to help to reduce global warming by producing electricity without polluting the atmosphere. As the wind turbine's long blades turn in the wind, they make electricity. The largest wind turbines are built in the sea off the coast.

Glossary

BEAUFORT SCALE Scale that measures the strength, or force, of a wind by its speed. The scale describes the effects of winds of different speeds and goes from force 0, which is no wind, to force 12, which is a hurricane.

CARBON DIOXIDE One of the gases in the air. Carbon dioxide is also produced when fuel is burned.

CONDENSE To change from a gas into a liquid.

CROPS Plants grown by farmers to be used in some way, for example, as food.

CYCLONE Any violent storm. Storms that are called hurricanes in other parts of the world are called cyclones in Australia, southern Asia and southeast Africa.

DEBRIS Garbage, fragments, and other things scattered by the wind, an explosion, or other event.

DESERT A region with little rain and few plants.

DOWNDRAFT Wind that blows downward toward the surface of the Earth.

DUST DEVIL A small tornado that sucks up dust as it moves across the land.

EQUATOR Imaginary line around the middle of the Earth, halfway between the North and South poles.

EVACUATE To leave a dangerous building or area to go to a safer place.

EYE (OF A HURRICANE) Area of calm at the center of a hurricane.

EYEWALL Clouds that surround the eye of a hurricane. The winds are strongest and the rain heaviest in the eyewall.

FLOOD Water covering land that is usually dry.

FLOOD DEFENCES Walls and other barriers built to stop water flooding.

FUJITA SCALE Scale that measures the strength of a tornado from the amount of damage it does.

FUNNEL Narrow tube; the funnel of a tornado is a narrow column of rising air surrounded by cloud.

GLOBAL WARMING Increase in the average temperature of the air around the Earth. Global warming is caused by an increase in gases, such as carbon dioxide, in the air.

GREENHOUSE GASES Gases in the air that trap the Sun's heat. Greenhouse gases include water vapor, carbon dioxide, and methane.

LEVEE Bank built to stop a river overflowing.

LIGHTNING Flash of light in the sky caused by a huge spark of electricity.

POWER LINE A heavy wire for carrying electricity.

PREVAILING WINDS Winds from a particular direction that normally blow over an area.

RADAR An electronic system that uses radio waves to pinpoint where an object is.

SAFFIR-SIMPSON SCALE Scale for measuring the strength of a hurricane by the speed of its winds.

SEWAGE Waste material and water from toilets and drains.

STORM CHASER Person who seeks out and follows storms, particularly tornadoes and hurricanes, to examine them close up.

STORM SURGE A rapid rise of sea level caused by storm winds pushing sea water toward the coast.

SUPERCELL THUNDERCLOUD A thundercloud with a very strong updraft.

THUNDER Loud noise made by a flash of lightning. The flash of lightning heats the air around it, making it suddenly expand.

THUNDERCLOUD Tall, dark cloud that can produce lightning and thunder.

TROPICAL Taking place in the tropics, the part of the world on each side of the Equator between the Tropic of Cancer and the Tropic of Capricorn.

TYPHOON Tropical storm that begins in the northwest Pacific Ocean and moves west, hitting countries from the Philippines to Japan.

UPDRAFT Wind that blows upward.

VALLEY Low land with mountains or hills on each side.

WATERSPOUT A tornado that moves across the sea or a lake, sucking up water.

WATER VAPOR Water in the form of a gas.

WEATHER SATELLITE Spacecraft that orbits the Earth, photographing clouds and measuring aspects of the weather.

Index